DISASTER RESILIENCE IN ASIA

A SPECIAL SUPPLEMENT OF ASIA'S JOURNEY TO PROSPERITY: POLICY, MARKET, AND TECHNOLOGY OVER 50 YEARS

JULY 2021

ASIAN DEVELOPMENT BANK

ADB

CONTENTS

TABLES, FIGURES, AND BOXES

PREFACE

In January 2020, the Asian Development Bank (ADB) published *Asia's Journey to Prosperity: Policy, Market, and Technology over 50 Years*. It offers an overview of Asia's growth and transformation over the past 50 years, and discusses the key policy lessons drawn from the region's continuing success. The book focuses on the role that policies, markets, and technology play in promoting structural transformation, human capital development, trade and investment, infrastructure, macroeconomic stability, poverty reduction, gender equality, environmental sustainability, development finance, and regional cooperation and integration. The sudden emergence of the coronavirus disease (COVID-19) and the ensuing pandemic underscored the importance of building disaster resilience, a topic of increasing relevance not specifically covered with its own chapter. This special supplement systematically addresses issues that are related to disaster resilience.

Asia has seen tremendous economic and social progress since the 1960s. By 2018, developing Asia's share of global output had grown to 24% from just 4% in 1960; those categorized as "extremely poor" had fallen to 173 million from 1.6 billion in 1981; and average life expectancy at birth grew to 72 years from 45 years in 1960. Yet, the region remains increasingly vulnerable to disaster risk. Over the years, developing Asia has seen a rising trend in disasters, many of which had cost lives and livelihoods, contributing to poverty and rising inequality.

The COVID-19 pandemic is testament to the debilitating effects that disasters can have on people, businesses, and economies. A year after the first case was recorded, COVID-19 had afflicted more than 80 million people globally, caused 1.8 million deaths, and set back global output by more than 2 years. Into its second year, the pandemic continues through its second and third waves of infections globally. ADB estimates suggest that global losses from the pandemic relative to a baseline without COVID-19 amount to 5.5%–8.7% of gross domestic product (GDP) in 2020 and 3.6%–6.3% of GDP in 2021. In developing Asia, the estimated losses are 6.0%–9.5% of regional GDP in 2020 and 3.6%–6.3% of GDP in 2021. The massive loss of life and economic output highlights the importance of addressing disaster risk and helping protect the development gains of the past 50 years.

This supplement updates Part 2 of the *Asian Development Outlook 2019: Strengthening Disaster Resilience* and the various ADB studies on the economic impact of COVID-19. The report was prepared by a team from the Economic Research and Regional Cooperation Department, supported by Lea Sumulong and Jade Tolentino, and edited by Guy Sacerdoti. Mary Ann Magadia facilitated the production process, with help from Judy Yñiguez, Ricardo Chan, Lawrence Casiraya, and Marjorie Celis. Anthony Victoria conceptualized the cover design. Staff from ADB's Department of Communications, including Ami Takagawa, Sarah O'Connor, and Cynthia Hidalgo, provided guidance on overall production and dissemination.

Yasuyuki Sawada
Chief Economist and Director General
Economic Research and
Regional Cooperation Department
Asian Development Bank

ABBREVIATIONS

ADB	Asian Development Bank
COVID-19	coronavirus disease
DRM	disaster risk management
DRR	disaster risk reduction
GDP	gross domestic product
MERS	Middle East respiratory syndrome
NPL	nonperforming loan
PRC	People's Republic of China
SARS	severe acute respiratory syndrome

INTRODUCTION

Despite Asia's dramatic economic progress since the 1960s, the region remains vulnerable to the threat of hazards turning into disasters. Continued exposure to a wide range of disaster risk—both from natural and technological or human-made hazards—can undermine the region's success in economic development and poverty reduction over the past 50 years. The global health and economic costs from the coronavirus disease (COVID-19) pandemic attests to the severe impact from these threats, and to what can be destabilizing if not catastrophic characteristics of disasters. As of 31 December 2020, COVID-19 had afflicted more than 80 million people worldwide, caused about 1.8 million deaths, and set back global economic output by at least 2.5 years.[1]

The widespread global effects from the pandemic show that disasters can destroy livelihoods and businesses, displace workers, and kill thousands of people. The impact is usually worse for developing economies, and for the most disadvantaged segments of society. Hence, there has been a growing awareness and acceptance in the region that understanding and addressing disaster risk are imperative to protect and sustain Asia's long-term development. And mitigating these risks necessitates a deep appreciation of the underlying context and relationships between the economy, society, and environment within which they occur.

Natural hazards become disasters when combined with the vulnerability and exposure of populations—harming human lives, activities, and properties. Vulnerability and exposure depend on various factors, such as poverty and inequality, urbanization, state of infrastructure, access to insurance, credit and other markets, and the unsustainable use of resources and ecosystems. Further, climate change heightens disaster risk as it changes the frequency, intensity, scope, and timing of severe weather events.

This special supplement focuses on disasters triggered by natural hazards. It is divided into two parts. The first is devoted to a discussion of disasters in general. It begins with a description of the generally rising trend

---

[1]   ADB COVID-19 Policy Database (accessed 16 January 2021).

of disaster risk in developing Asia[2] since the 1960s, before dissecting the high human cost of disasters. It then discusses the drivers of disaster risk, followed by an examination of the region's risk management and disaster resilience efforts over the past few decades.

The second part delves into how the region is navigating the ill effects of the COVID-19 pandemic. It begins with the evolution and current state of the pandemic globally. It then discusses its economic impact through 2021. It also describes policy responses by governments and the Asian Development Bank (ADB). The special supplement concludes with policy lessons of disaster resilience that developing Asian economies can gain from each other's individual and collective experiences. Regional economies can carry these lessons forward to accelerate recovery and, hopefully, build back greener, from one of the worst global health crises in recent history, and prepare them for future disaster risks.

---

[2] Developing Asia consists of Asia excluding Australia, Japan, and New Zealand. Asia consists of the 48 regional members of ADB.

PART 1: DISASTERS

This section updates and expands on Part 2 of Asian Development Bank (ADB). 2019a. *Asian Development Outlook 2019: Strengthening Disaster Resilience*. Manila.

Chapter I

RISING TREND OF DISASTER RISK

Over the past 50 years, many hazards have become risks that eventually materialized into disasters. Asia's exposure to a wide range of natural and human-made hazards resulted in numerous disasters that cost the region and its people huge losses—in lives, livelihoods, and properties. Although the region has improved in terms of disaster preparedness, the threat that natural hazards will become disasters persists. History is full of disasters that quickly wiped out years of progress, whether in economic development or poverty reduction. Most recently, just a year after the first coronavirus disease (COVID-19) case was recorded, the health and economic costs from the pandemic continue to pile up. The global economy is estimated to have contracted by 3.5% in 2020,[3] with developing Asia's economies down by 0.4%.[4] COVID-19 is projected to have pushed 78 million–162 million people in developing Asia into poverty.[5]

Hazards can be either natural or human-made.[6] Natural hazards occur suddenly with little or no warning, or can build up slowly over time. When ignited by a population's exposure or vulnerability, they become disasters. Disasters may originate from different types of hazards. They can be geophysical, such as earthquakes, dry mass movements, or volcanic activities. They can be weather-related—climatological (droughts and wildfires), hydrological (floods and landslides), or meteorological (storms and extreme temperatures). And they can be biological (animal accidents,

---

[3] International Monetary Fund. 2021. *World Economic Outlook Update, January 2021.* Washington, DC.

[4] ADB. 2020a. *Asian Development Outlook 2020 Supplement: Paths Diverge in Recovery from the Pandemic.* Manila (December).

[5] ADB. 2020b. *Asian Development Outlook 2020 Update: Wellness in Worrying Times.* Manila; and J. Bulan et al. 2020. COVID-19 and Poverty: Some Scenarios. Manila (unpublished note prepared for the Economic Research and Regional Cooperation Department, ADB).

[6] The term "natural disaster" may not be entirely caused by nature, but by a combination of natural hazards and human behavior that increases exposure or vulnerability (World Bank and United Nations. 2010. *Natural Hazards, UnNatural Disasters: The Economics of Effective Prevention.* Washington, DC). With this caveat, we follow the Emergency Events Database (EM-DAT) and common practice when using the term "natural disaster" and other related terminologies (e.g., biological, climatological, geophysical, hydrophysical, and meteorological disasters).

epidemics, or insect infestations). Disasters emanating from technology, on the other hand, are human-made—whether industrial, transport-related, or miscellaneous accidents. Broadly speaking, economic crises and violence-related extreme events are also considered disasters.[7] Economic crises can contract output; cause famine; hyperinflation; or result in financial, currency, or debt crises—such as the 1997–1998 Asian Financial Crisis and the 2008–2009 Global Financial Crisis (Chapter 10 in *Asia's Journey to Prosperity: Policy, Market, and Technology over 50 Years*).[8] Violence-related disasters include terrorist attacks, civil wars, and international wars. In addition, multiple disasters are often compounded. One recent example was the 2011 Great East Japan Earthquake and Tsunami, during which a geological disaster caused the Fukushima nuclear power plant technological disaster. In this special supplement, we deal with events triggered by natural hazards.

Available data show that, from 1960 to 2005, disasters triggered by natural and technological hazards increased across developing Asia in terms of national average disaster occurrence per year (Figure 1).[9] Globally, the number of disasters per country peaked in 2005, but has generally slowed since. A similar pattern can be seen in the average disaster occurrence in developing Asia. Between 1960 and 1975, nearly all disasters originated from natural hazards. Human-made disasters began to increase starting in the late 1980s up through 2017, though incidence has since decreased.

Since the 1960s, about one-third of recorded disasters triggered by natural hazards worldwide occurred in developing Asia (Table 1). By decade, the region's share of these disasters has remained steady at 34%–40%. However, the distribution of people affected has been disproportionately large—at least four of five people affected by natural hazards live in developing Asia. Indeed, between 1960 and 2020, the region accounted for 85% of affected persons, 65% of those who died, and 27% of the damage cost from global disasters triggered by natural hazards (the low share of damage

---

[7]   Y. Sawada. 2007. The impact of natural and manmade disasters on household welfare. *Agricultural Economics*. 37 (s1): pp. 59–73.

[8]   ADB. 2020. *Asia's Journey to Prosperity: Policy, Market, and Technology over 50 Years*. Tokyo.

[9]   Data are sourced from EM-DAT: The Emergency Events Database - Université Catholique de Louvain (UCL) - CRED, D. Guha-Sapir - www.emdat.be, Brussels, Belgium. Data before 2000 are less reliable than data from 2000 onward. Data on epidemics throughout this publication are underreported as the database does not capture events that develop gradually over time.

Figure 1. Disaster Occurrence, Developing Asia, 1960–2020
(annual average)

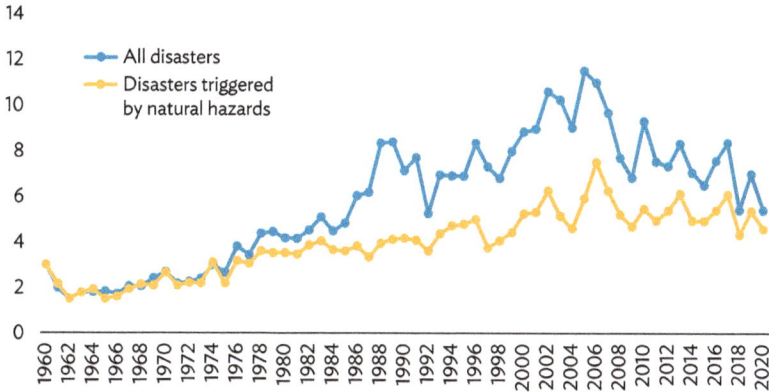

Notes: Disasters are either triggered by natural hazards or by human-made hazards.. Figures are simple averages of the number of disasters in developing Asian economies with at least one disaster per year.

Source: Asian Development Bank estimates using EM-DAT: The Emergency Events Database - Université Catholique de Louvain (UCL) - CRED, D. Guha-Sapir - www.emdat.be (accessed 25 January 2021). Brussels, Belgium.

Table 1: Percentage of Global Disasters in Developing Asia by Decade, 1960–2020

	1960–1969	1970–1979	1980–1989	1990–1999	2000–2009	2010–2020	1960–2020
Death toll	95	70	14	56	76	18	65
Number affected	84	86	87	88	89	75	85
Damage	6	24	16	28	30	25	27
Total incidents	35	40	36	35	34	37	36

Note: The figures only include disasters triggered by natural hazards.

Source: Asian Development Bank estimates using EM-DAT: The Emergency Events Database - Université Catholique de Louvain (UCL) - CRED, D. Guha-Sapir - www.emdat.be (accessed 25 January 2021). Brussels, Belgium.

cost is perhaps because of the region's relatively low income and property valuation levels).[10]

Among the region's disasters triggered by natural hazards, 82% were weather-related (5% climatological, 43% hydrological, and 34% meteorological); 12% geophysical; and 6% biological. The most common weather-related disasters are from floods and storms. However, over the past 6 decades, disasters emanating from climatological hazards accounted for the largest number of deaths in developing Asia, despite their low frequency among various types of disasters (Figure 2). The large number of deaths occurred between 1965 and 1967, when India suffered from twin droughts that affected nearly the entire country and created widespread famine—1.5 million

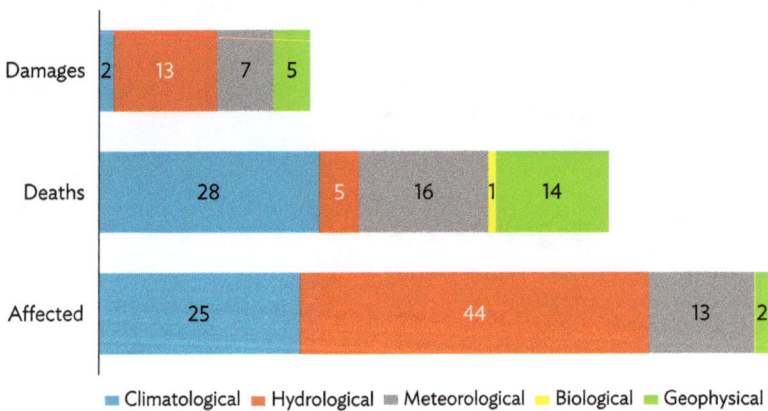

Figure 2. **Percentage of Global Disasters in Developing Asia by Type of Disaster, 1960–2020**

Notes: Climatological disasters include droughts and wildfires; hydrological disasters include floods and landslides; meteorological disasters include storms and extreme temperatures; biological disasters include animal accidents, epidemics, and insect infestations; and geophysical disasters include earthquakes, dry mass movements, and volcanic activities.

Source: Asian Development Bank estimates using EM-DAT: The Emergency Events Database - Université Catholique de Louvain (UCL) - CRED, D. Guha-Sapir – www.emdat.be (accessed 25 January 2021). Brussels, Belgium.

---

[10] In general, richer nations suffer greater economic losses from disasters than poorer countries, as the value of damaged assets is far larger even if the physical intensity is comparable. Y. Sawada and Y. Takasaki. 2017. Natural Disaster, Poverty, and Development: An Introduction. *World Development* 94 (C): pp. 2–15.

people died during that calamity. Regional deaths from meteorological hazards are large because of the greater frequency of storms in developing Asia. Deaths from geophysical hazards are also significant, often because of their unpredictable nature (such as earthquakes). They account for more than one-fifth of all deaths in developing Asia during 1960–2020. Hydrological disasters, meanwhile, have had the most devastating impact in terms of people harmed (for example, through physical injury or temporary displacement) and damage costs.

Across various subregions in developing Asia, disasters during 1960–2020 were most frequent in Southeast Asia, followed by South Asia, East Asia, the Pacific, and Central Asia. The least number of disaster occurrences was in Central Asia, as records only began in the 1990s. In Central Asia, South Asia, and Southeast Asia, disasters from hydrological events were the most common, accounting for 57%, 50%, and 45%, respectively (Figure 3). In the Pacific and East Asia, meteorological hazards triggered the greatest number of disasters.

Figure 3. **Distribution of Disaster Occurrence by Subregion, 1960–2020**

(% of total)

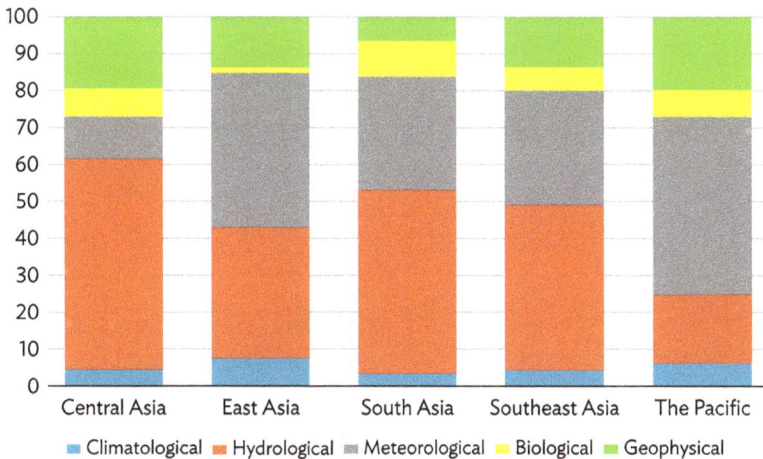

Source: Asian Development Bank estimates using EM-DAT: The Emergency Events Database - Université Catholique de Louvain (UCL) - CRED, D. Guha-Sapir – www.emdat.be (accessed 25 January 2021). Brussels, Belgium.

Nevertheless, the United Nations Office for Disaster Risk Reduction points out that mortality from "extensive disaster risk"—frequent (but often not severe) weather-related events—is not measured fully. And it has also been increasing.[11] It is important to note that households, micro and small enterprises, and local governments often bear the brunt of losses from these events—and thus the value of damage cited in international reports likely underestimate actual numbers. For these kinds of risks, the most meaningful response may be investing in disaster-resilient infrastructure and building community resilience through education and strengthened social support.

---

[11]   United Nations Office for Disaster Risk Reduction. 2017. *Words into Action Guidelines: Build Back Better in Recovery, Rehabilitation and Reconstruction – Consultative Version*. Geneva.

Chapter II

THE TREMENDOUS COST OF DISASTERS

Disasters affect developing and developed economies alike, but there is often significantly more damage inflicted on developing economies. Developing Asia is the most vulnerable region in the world. Between 2000 and 2020, disasters triggered by natural hazards claimed at least 36,000 lives annually in developing Asia, more than half of fatalities globally. For every five people affected by these disasters worldwide, four were from developing Asia.[12] And of the $135 billion in average annual global damage, more than one-fourth accrued to the region.

The effects of disasters are often local and short-term, but as a previous Asian Development Bank (ADB) study shows, they can creep into other locations and continue for a long time.[13] Those burdened most from these impacts are the poor, the marginalized, and the isolated. Without preventive action, the havoc wreaked from the most severe disasters remain not just life-threatening, but also poverty-inducing.[14]

A.   Short-Term and Local Effects of Disasters

Disasters are often localized events with the affected area accounting for most of the financial damage. However, much of the previous literature on disaster effects dwells on the macroeconomic or regional impact, leading to missed opportunities when designing policies for building local resilience. This is unfortunate, given the often substantial immediate economic effects of disasters on local economic activity. An ADB study, for example, using nightlight intensity as a proxy for economic activity, finds that tropical storms in the Philippines can reduce local economic activity in the year

---

[12] "Affected," as defined in EM-DAT, covers everything from physical injury to temporary displacement (because of a disaster such as a flood, even if it causes little damage).

[13] ADB. 2019a. *Asian Development Outlook 2019: Strengthening Disaster Resilience.* Manila.

[14] Y. Sawada and Y. Takasaki. 2017. Natural Disaster, Poverty, and Development: An Introduction. *World Development* 94 (C): pp. 2–15.

Box 1. The Death Toll from Disasters in Asia

In developing Asia, the most deadly disasters since 1990 can be found in Southeast Asia, South Asia, and East Asia. The region's highest death tolls—more than 220,000 from the Indian Ocean earthquake and tsunami in December 2004 (73% of which were from Indonesia); almost 140,000 each from cyclones in Bangladesh and Myanmar in late April–early May in 1991; close to 90,000 in the May 2008 earthquake in the People's Republic of China; and more than 70,000 during the 2005 earthquake in Pakistan—clearly show the region's disproportionate share of total deaths worldwide (Box Table and Box Figure).

Box Table: Most Devastating Disasters in Developing Asia, 1990–2020
(number of fatalities)

	Event	Country	Deaths	Year	Date
1.	2004 Indian Ocean Earthquake and Tsunami	Various	226,096	2004	26 December
		Indonesia	165,708		
		Sri Lanka	35,399		
		India	16,389		
		Thailand	8,345		
		Maldives	102		
		Malaysia	80		
		Myanmar	71		
		Bangladesh	2		
2.	Cyclone Gorky	Bangladesh	138,866	1991	29 April–10 May
3.	Cyclone Nargis	Myanmar	138,366	2008	2–3 May
4.	2008 Great Sichuan or Wenchuan Earthquake	People's Republic of China	87,476	2008	12 May
5.	2005 Earthquake	Various	74,648	2005	8 October
		Pakistan	73,338	2005	
		India	1,309	2005	
		Afghanistan	1	2005	
6.	2001 Gujarat Earthquake	Various	20,017	2001	26 January
		India	20,005	2001	
		Pakistan	12	2001	

continued on next page

Box 1 *continued*

	Event	Country	Deaths	Year	Date
7.	Tropical Cyclone and Flood	India	9,843	1999	28–30 October
8.	Earthquake	India	9,748	1993	29 September
9.	Earthquake	Nepal	8,831	2015	25 April
10.	Typhoon Haiyan (Yolanda)	Philippines	7,354	2013	8 November
11.	Flood	India	6,054	2013	12–27 June

Source: Asian Development Bank estimates using EM-DAT: The Emergency Events Database - Université Catholique de Louvain (UCL) - CRED, D. Guha-Sapir - www.emdat.be (accessed 25 January 2021), Brussels, Belgium.

Box Figure. Deaths from Weather- and Nonweather-Related Disasters in Developing Asia,1990–2020
('000)

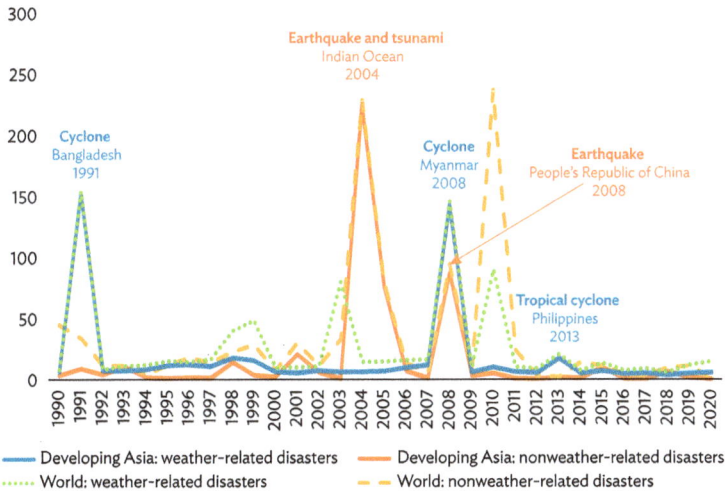

Source: Asian Development Bank estimates using EM-DAT: The Emergency Events Database - Université Catholique de Louvain (UCL) - CRED, D. Guha-Sapir – www.emdat.be (accessed 25 January 2021), Brussels, Belgium.

that it occurs by 1.7% on average.[15] In the most severe cases, losses can be as high as 23%. From 1990 to 2020, the total impact from storms in the Philippines reached at least $20 billion.

These local effects are often short-lived, partly because of the fact that households temporarily evacuate affected areas, then return later. The quick recovery from these local events is consistent with a recent study on the local effects of flooding, where massive floods in urban areas can reduce gross domestic product (GDP) by 2%–8% annually.[16] Similar to the typhoon study on the Philippines, the recent study on floods finds that changes in economic activity in cities affected by flooding are not permanent, lasting just up to 1 year or less. Other well-cited studies for other Asian economies found a similar qualitative result for earthquakes and short-lived human-made disasters, such as the Allied bombing of cities during World War II in Japan.[17] Similarly, bombing during the Vietnam war also did not create long-term poverty traps.[18]

This relatively rapid restoration of economic livelihoods and activity should not, however, be viewed as a sign of disaster resilience, especially for vulnerable places where disasters occur frequently. If nothing further is done except the restoration of activity, returning to these affected areas simply means placing the same populations and assets back in the path of disasters.

Further, in the coming years, climate change is expected to worsen the intensity and impact of disasters, especially in vulnerable locations. For small countries, more extreme events mean more massive damage affecting wider swathes of the population. For instance, in 2015, Cyclone Pam—the second-strongest tropical cyclone in the South Pacific—reduced Vanuatu's GDP that year by 64%.

---

[15]   E. Strobl. 2019. The Impact of Typhoons on Economic Activity in the Philippines: Evidence from Nightlight Intensity. *ADB Economics Working Paper Series* No. 589. Manila: ADB (July).

[16]   A. Kocornik-Mina et al. 2020. Flooded Cities. *American Economic Journal: Applied Economics.* 12 (2): pp. 35–66.

[17]   D. R. Davis and D. E. Weinstein. 2002. Bones, Bombs, and Break Points: The Geography of Economic Activity. *American Economic Review.* 92 (5): pp. 1269–1289.

[18]   E. Miguel and G. Roland. 2011. The Long-run Impact of Bombing Vietnam. *Journal of Development Economics.* 96 (1): pp. 1–15.

B.   Long-Term and Ripple Effects of Disasters

While most disasters have short-term local effects, severe disasters wield more persistent damage. Economic recovery can also be slow or incomplete for areas where there is little diversity in employment, production, and trade. In the Hyogo Prefecture in Japan after the 1995 Kobe earthquake, for example, income per capita in 2005 was at least 10% below its level 10 years previously.[19]

Small island developing economies, such as those in the Pacific, are particularly vulnerable because their size is often dwarfed by the magnitude of a disaster (Figure 4). These disasters can destroy critical infrastructure (such as airports), fracturing prospects for an immediate economic revival. Lack of diversity in production and exports makes it difficult for these countries to recover both in the short and long term, similar to what happened in Haiti after it suffered a 7.0-magnitude earthquake in 2010.

Figure 4. **Damage from Disasters, 2000–2019**
(% of GDP, unweighted average)

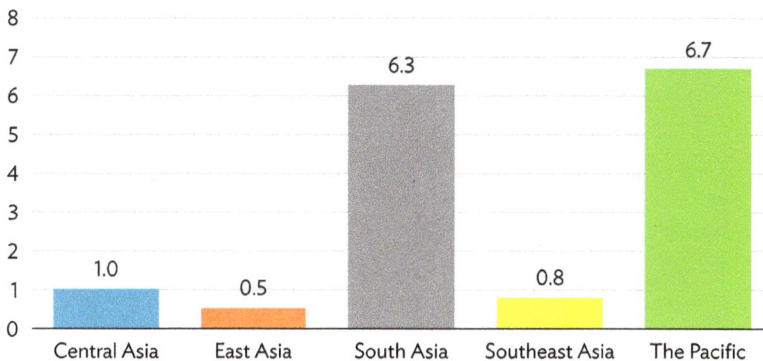

GDP = gross domestic product.

Source: Asian Development Bank estimates using EM-DAT: The Emergency Events Database - Université Catholique de Louvain (UCL) - CRED, D. Guha-Sapir – www.emdat.be (accessed 25 January 2021). Brussels, Belgium.

---

[19] W. duPont IV et al. 2015. The Long-Run Socio-Economic Consequences of a Disaster: The 1995 Earthquake in Kobe. *PLoS ONE*. 10 (10): e0138714.

Disaster effects can also persist because of their indirect impacts through market prices. After the 2011 floods in Thailand, the top manufacturers of the country's hard disk drive industry were found to have colluded, as the average price of hard disks returned to their pre-disaster levels to a limited extent, before driving higher prices from late 2011 onward.[20]

Some disaster effects are more pervasive, spreading across geographic areas via supply chain linkages and the migration of people (including employees). Disruptions in supply chains caused by a disaster not only impact firms in the affected area, but also firms across the world linked to their production networks. The 2011 Thailand floods and the Tohoku earthquake in Japan in the same year both showed how disasters propagate their impacts by limiting inputs needed by firms elsewhere. One study found that, after the 2011 earthquake and tsunami, Japan's GDP declined by as much as 1.2% because of negative spillover effects via input–output linkages.[21]

Further, the effects from disasters permeate to another sector of the economy—households and individuals—and they do so in many interlinking ways. Families impacted by disasters use up their savings or take out loans at high interest rates, usually from informal lenders, leading to mounting household debt and poverty traps. Spending on disaster and rebuilding costs (such as house repairs and hospital fees for injured family members) can also lead to reduced household spending on food, health, and education. In addition, if these households include children, their potential can be reduced, even later in life. Children orphaned by the Indonesia tsunami in 2004, for example, later completed fewer years of schooling because of either loss-related trauma or assumed parental tasks.[22] In other regions, research shows that pregnant women exposed to

[20] H. Nakata, Y. Sawada, and N. Wakamori. 2020. Robustness of Production Networks Against Economic Disasters: Thailand Case. In V. Anbumozhi, F. Kimura, and S. Thangavelu (eds). *Supply Chain Resilience*. Singapore: Springer.

[21] V. M. Carvalho et al. 2021. Supply Chain Disruptions: Evidence from the Great East Japan Earthquake. *Quarterly Journal of Economics*. 136 (2): pp. 1255–1321.

[22] A. G. Cas et al. 2014. The Impact of Parental Death on Child Well-being: Evidence from the Indian Ocean Tsunami. *Demography*. 51 (2): pp. 437–457.

a catastrophic event bore offspring with lower birth weights[23] or had lower educational attainment later.[24]

Disasters also cause people to abandon affected areas, creating displaced populations. In 2017, about three-fifths of those displaced worldwide were from East Asia, Southeast Asia, and South Asia. Migration because of climate change is also expected to rise quickly. Further, disasters expose displaced populations not only to natural hazard risks but to serious health risks as well, such as widespread disease. In Dhaka, Bangladesh, for example, one study found that the increase in hospitalizations because of dengue fever can be linked to flooding or factors associated with high and low river levels.[25]

---

[23] M. Hyland and J. Russ. 2019. Water as Destiny—The Long-term Impacts of Drought in Sub-Saharan Africa. *World Development*. 115 (C): pp. 30–45.

[24] G. Caruso and S. Miller. 2015. Long Run Effects and Intergenerational Transmission of Natural Disasters: A Case Study on the 1970 Ancash Earthquake. *Journal of Development Economics*. 117 (C): pp. 134–150.

[25] M. Hashizume et al. 2012. Hydroclimatological variability and dengue transmission in Dhaka, Bangladesh: a time-series study. *BMC Infectious Diseases*. 12: p. 98.

Chapter III
DRIVERS OF DISASTER RISK

Generally speaking, a disaster occurs when a hazard interacts with an exposed and vulnerable population, harming people, damaging physical assets such as property and infrastructure, and with indirect losses from lost economic activity. In developing Asia, exposure to disaster risk has risen over the past 50 years because of growing populations and higher economic growth. The region's economic transformation has led to a greater concentration of assets and people in high-risk locations, including coastal areas and densely populated megacities. This has led to more people and property congregating in the path of potential disasters. Indeed, during the 2011 flood in Greater Bangkok, the protracted floods submerged Thailand's primary industrial estates, affected 950,000 people, and incurred more than $46.5 billion in damage,[26] making it the costliest flood ever documented globally.[27]

In very extreme natural hazards, exposure often plays an even larger role than vulnerability in determining the extent of disaster risk. For example, tsunamis sweep across all properties and populations in affected areas, regardless of inhabitants' income, race, or social class.

Higher-income economies with stronger institutions, however, tend to have lower vulnerability to disasters, particularly when they can prepare ahead of time, and especially in reducing the number of fatalities.[28] Meanwhile, poverty increases vulnerability, and is intricately linked with other underlying factors, making it both a driver and a consequence of disaster risk.

---

[26] World Bank. 2012. *Thai Flood 2011: Rapid Assessment for Resilient Recovery and Reconstruction Planning.* Bangkok.

[27] EM-DAT: The Emergency Events Database - Université Catholique de Louvain (UCL) - CRED, D. Guha-Sapir - www.emdat.be (accessed 25 January 2021), Brussels, Belgium.

[28] M. E. Kahn. 2005. The Death Toll from Natural Disasters: The Role of Income, Geography, and Institutions. *Review of Economics and Statistics.* 87 (2): pp. 271–284.

Rapid economic progress in Asia and the Pacific has made the region more susceptible to disaster risk. Some of its unintended consequences—uneven economic development, environmental degradation, and climate change—along with weak governance, can intensify the underlying drivers of disaster risk. These include poor urban and local planning; ecosystem damage (for example, destruction of wetlands, mangroves, and forests); and high levels of poverty (Figure 5). These factors are interlinked—so addressing them will lower disaster risk, address climate change, and promote environmental sustainability.[29]

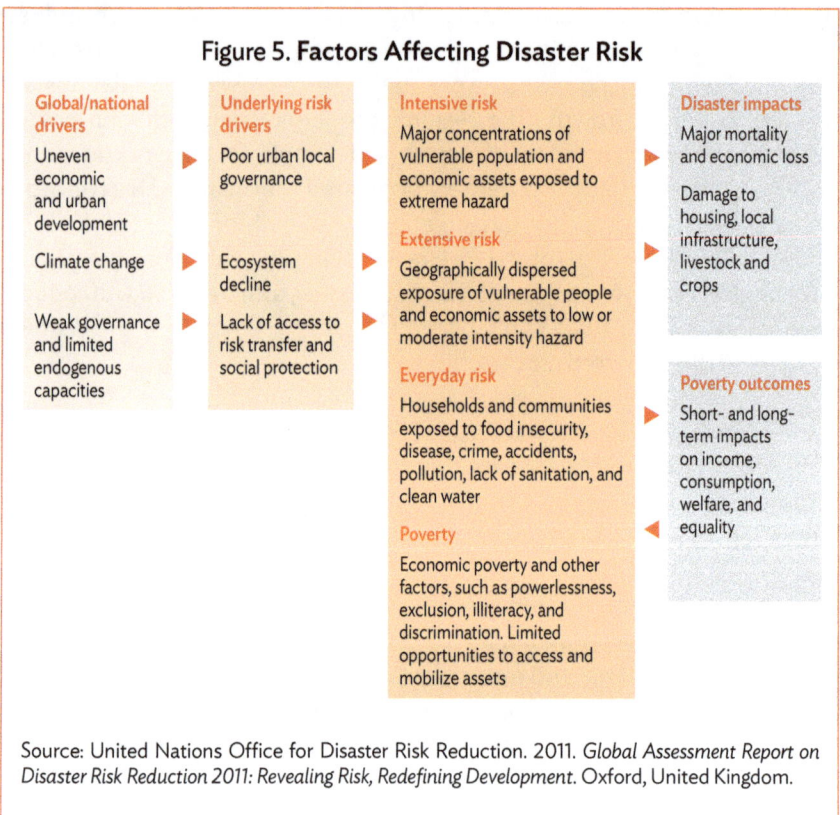

Figure 5. Factors Affecting Disaster Risk

Global/national drivers	Underlying risk drivers	Intensive risk	Disaster impacts
Uneven economic and urban development	Poor urban local governance	Major concentrations of vulnerable population and economic assets exposed to extreme hazard	Major mortality and economic loss
		Extensive risk	Damage to housing, local infrastructure, livestock and crops
Climate change	Ecosystem decline	Geographically dispersed exposure of vulnerable people and economic assets to low or moderate intensity hazard	
Weak governance and limited endogenous capacities	Lack of access to risk transfer and social protection		
		Everyday risk	**Poverty outcomes**
		Households and communities exposed to food insecurity, disease, crime, accidents, pollution, lack of sanitation, and clean water	Short- and long-term impacts on income, consumption, welfare, and equality
		Poverty	
		Economic poverty and other factors, such as powerlessness, exclusion, illiteracy, and discrimination. Limited opportunities to access and mobilize assets	

Source: United Nations Office for Disaster Risk Reduction. 2011. *Global Assessment Report on Disaster Risk Reduction 2011: Revealing Risk, Redefining Development.* Oxford, United Kingdom.

Looking at Figure 5, several points are worth highlighting. Poor households are likely to be less resilient than their rich counterparts because of the former's limited access to insurance mechanisms and adequate

---

[29] United Nations Office for Disaster Risk Reduction. 2011. *Global Assessment Report on Disaster Risk Reduction 2011: Revealing Risk, Redefining Development.* Oxford, United Kingdom.

safety nets, either on account of unavailability or unaffordability. Disasters have long-term effects on vulnerable populations, including human capital (especially for children and women), thus propagating chronic poverty and creating poverty traps. Informal settlers in urban areas, whose numbers increase every year, also face this vulnerability. Climate change amplifies these effects in two ways: it not only magnifies weather disturbances and other hazards, but also reduces the ability of poor populations to recover from massive disaster costs.

A growing understanding of these relationships is helping authorities design good strategies that strengthen the disaster resilience of poor communities and other vulnerable populations.

Chapter IV

ASIA'S DISASTER RESILIENCE AND RISK MANAGEMENT OVER THE PAST 50 YEARS

A. Why Is Disaster Resilience Important?

A United Nations Working Group defines "resilience" as "the ability of a system, community, or society exposed to hazards to resist, absorb, accommodate, adapt to, transform, and recover from the effects of a hazard in a timely and efficient manner."[30] As the negative effects of a disaster can persist over time and also transmit to other locations, strengthening disaster resilience is key to managing disaster risk.

The starting point for building disaster resilience is by reducing risk. Disaster risk reduction (DRR) in turn entails diminishing vulnerability and exposure to natural hazards that are at the highest risk of becoming disasters, whether as local events or major catastrophes.

To be effective, confronting the drivers of disaster risk and vulnerability requires adopting management strategies that give importance to preventive, comprehensive, and integrated measures. This conceptual shift toward a culture of resilience is crucial to ensure better planning and to prevent incurring large losses (such as deaths, damaged infrastructure, and loss of livelihood). Moreover, apart from this possible reduction in disaster costs, two other dividends from investing in disaster resilience have been increasingly recognized in recent literature.[31] First, it can unlock development (by encouraging household savings, entrepreneurship, and firm innovation); and, second, it can produce co-benefits (through positive economic, social, and environmental externalities).

The recent global paradigm shift toward disaster resilience is accompanied by an exploration of risk management strategies for

---

[30] The United Nations Intergovernmental Expert Working Group on Indicators and Terminology is tasked with clarifying the central concepts that guide the Sendai Framework priorities.

[31] For example, refer to Swenja Surminski and Thomas Tanner (eds). 2016. *Realising the 'Triple Dividend of Resilience': A New Business Case for Disaster Risk Management*. Berlin: Springer.

and participated by local communities and households. Community participation and empowerment allow both a shift in attitude and build the capacity of populations who are often at the front end of disasters.

Globally, significant achievements have been made in the thinking and practice of disaster risk management (DRM) over the past few decades, with developing Asia showing very visible progress.

B.   Overview of Disaster Resilience and Management in Asia

Over the past 20 years, Asia has begun to pay increasing attention to disaster management as the frequency of disasters and the magnitude of impacts rise. During this period, the region also made much progress in integrating DRR into national development plans. The approach to disaster management and later emphasis on disaster resilience has evolved over the years to meet Asia's pressing challenges, including hazards brought about by climate change. International thinking on disasters has also advanced from previous perceptions of disasters as unpreventable "acts of God" to the current view of disasters as development impediments that must be avoided and managed (Figure 6).

Throughout history, several developing Asian economies have often studied or followed in Japan's footsteps in the hope of carving out their own pathway toward progress and advancement (Chapter 2 in *Asia's Journey to Prosperity: Policy, Market, and Technology over 50 Years*). But the more pragmatic of them have also looked at Japan as a world leader in disaster risk preparedness. Learning from the 1923 Tokyo earthquake (which killed about 100,000 people) and responding to the immense damage caused by typhoon Ise-wan in 1959, Japan institutionalized DRR measures through a series of relevant regulations enacted in the 1960s.[32] Since then, as one of the most natural hazard-prone countries in the world, Japan has continuously fine-tuned its DRR strategies, often by using the latest tools in science and technology. With its advanced early warning systems and earthquake-proof

---

[32] These include Disaster Countermeasures Basic Act, the Soil Conservation and Flood Control Urgent Measures Act (1960); the establishment of the Central Disaster Management Council (1962); Act on Special Finance Support to Deal with Extremely Severe Disasters (1962); a Basic Disaster Management Plan (1963); and Act on Earthquake Insurance (1966); ADB. 2016. *Disaster Risk in Asia and the Pacific: Assessment, Management, and Finance.* Manila; and Government of Japan, Cabinet Office. 2015. *Disaster Management in Japan.* Tokyo.

Figure 6. Evolving Approaches to Disaster Risk Management

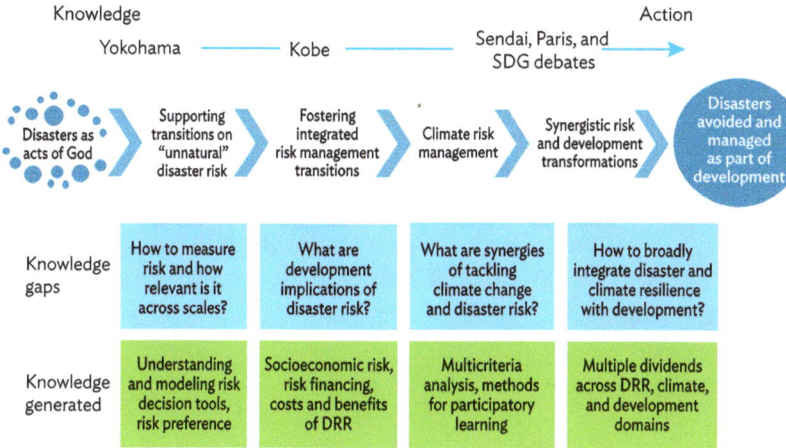

Knowledge

Yokohama ——— Kobe ——— Sendai, Paris, and
SDG debates

Action

Disasters as acts of God	Supporting transitions on "unnatural" disaster risk	Fostering integrated risk management transitions	Climate risk management	Synergistic risk and development transformations	Disasters avoided and managed as part of development

Knowledge gaps	How to measure risk and how relevant is it across scales?	What are development implications of disaster risk?	What are synergies of tackling climate change and disaster risk?	How to broadly integrate disaster and climate resilience with development?
Knowledge generated	Understanding and modeling risk decision tools, risk preference	Socioeconomic risk, risk financing, costs and benefits of DRR	Multicriteria analysis, methods for participatory learning	Multiple dividends across DRR, climate, and development domains

DRR = disaster risk reduction, SDG = Sustainable Development Goal.
Source: R. Mechler and S. Hochrainer-Stigler. 2019. Generating Multiple Resilience Dividends from Managing Unnatural Disasters in Asia: Opportunities for Measurement and Policy. *ADB Economics Working Paper* Series No. 601. Manila: ADB (December).

structures, Japan is one of the best-equipped countries to handle disaster risk. More importantly, disaster prevention has also been deeply ingrained into the populations' psyche, with citizen training in DRR starting early in school.

Globally, it was not until several decades later that the international community paid more serious attention to DRR. From 1994 to 2015, three global DRR conferences were held in Japan. In 1994, the first World Conference on Disaster Reduction adopted the Yokohama Strategy for a Safer World, which set out landmark guidelines for natural disaster prevention, preparedness, and mitigation. Eleven years later, 168 governments agreed to adopt the Hyogo Framework for Action, a blueprint for reducing disaster risk by 2015. It took stock of the progress that countries have made in implementing the Yokohama Strategy, and recommended a more proactive DRR approach, especially at the community level.

A more recent initiative is the Sendai Framework for Disaster Risk Reduction 2015–2030, a successor to the Hyogo Framework for Action. Adopted by 187 United Nations members at the Third World Conference on Disaster Risk Reduction in 2015, it provides countries with more concrete ways to build resilience and reduce disaster risk. To meet these objectives, the Sendai Framework emphasizes four key goals: (i) understanding disaster risk, (ii) strengthening disaster risk governance, (iii) investing in DRR, and (iv) enhancing disaster risk preparedness.

The Sendai Framework complements two major international agreements on climate change and development, also adopted in 2015: the Paris Agreement and the Sustainable Development Goals. All three initiatives (including the Sendai Framework) incorporate disaster and climate risk in addressing development challenges. By doing so they promote ways to simultaneously reduce disaster risk, adapt to climate change, and reap development dividends.

These developments highlight the remarkable progress in recent global donor commitment to disaster reduction. In developing Asia, humanitarian aid received for disaster prevention and preparedness dramatically increased—from $3.0 million (in constant 2018 dollars) in 2004 to $1.0 billion in 2019—making up one-third of all spending in humanitarian aid in 2019 (Figure 7). Donor disbursements allocated for disaster prevention and preparedness began to account for a larger proportion of total humanitarian aid beginning in 2012, when its share

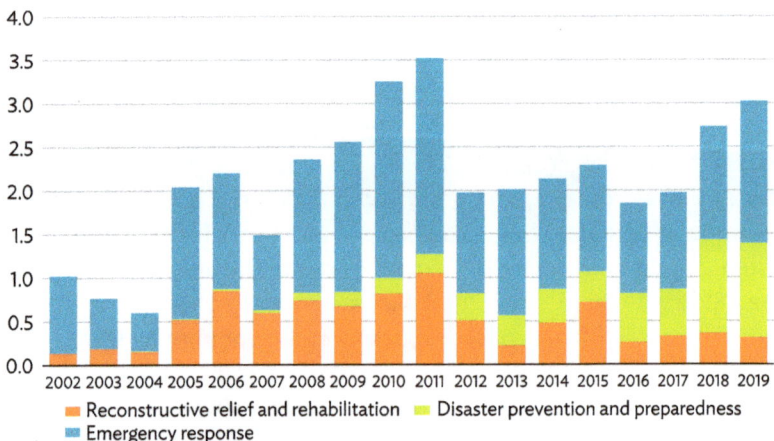

Figure 7. **Humanitarian Aid to Developing Asia, 2002–2019**
($ billion, 2018 prices)

Source: Organisation for Economic Co-operation and Development. *Humanitarian Assistance.* http://www.oecd.org/dac/stats/humanitarian-assistance.htm (accessed 28 January 2021).

increased into double digits. Overall, from 2012 to 2019, 25% of average yearly humanitarian aid to developing Asia was allocated for disaster prevention and preparedness spending, compared with 3% between 2004 and 2011. The rest was spent on reconstruction relief and rehabilitation along with emergency response. Since records began in 2002, the largest share of humanitarian aid has always gone to emergency response efforts.

There has also been progress in incorporating DRR in infrastructure planning and investment, reflecting the increasing recognition that there are multiple dividends to be gained from building resilience. ADB has supported developing Asian economies in this area, adopting a risk management approach to infrastructure planning and implementation that accentuates investing in infrastructure for disaster resilience, and increasing the resilience of infrastructure investments. It has also been helping its regional members implement other solutions for building climate- and disaster-resilient infrastructure, through working with governments in updating engineering standards and in providing DRR financing solutions and strategies.[33]

However, much work remains to be done. The infrastructure spending requirements for developing Asia—including those for climate change mitigation and adaptation—continue to be sizable ($26 trillion or $1.7 trillion annually from 2016 to 2030).[34] The enormity of the region's financing needs to meet its infrastructure gap highlights the importance of these investments and their role in influencing the exposure and vulnerability of the region to disaster risk. Most large urban infrastructure projects are irreversible or costly to undo. Hence, planning and investing in climate-friendly and disaster-resilient infrastructure—taking into account disaster risks in the location, design, construction, and implementation of an infrastructure project—can be a cost-effective way to reduce disaster risk.

Another way to reduce the cost of disasters (especially those pertaining to large, residual risks) is through insurance mechanisms. In Asia, the range of options for market and nonmarket insurance available to protect populations from the financial toll of disasters has widened over the years, though the degree of availability may differ for each mechanism

---

[33] X. Lu. 2019. Building Resilient Infrastructure for the Future: Background Paper for the G20 Climate Sustainability Working Group. *ADB Sustainable Development Working Paper Series* No. 61. Manila: ADB (July).

[34] ADB. 2017. *Meeting Asia's Infrastructure Needs*. Manila.

and for each economy. Broad market-based insurance mechanisms are not confined to insurance products in a narrow sense, but include, for example, agriculture insurance, microinsurance, disaster risk transfer products, disaster risk pooling funds, catastrophe bonds, and credit transactions (through banks and other financial institutions) which can act effectively as insurance for those affected to cope with disaster losses. The labor market also acts as an insurance mechanism when extra labor participation and earnings (such as from hiring disaster victims through post-disaster workfare programs) cover some of the economic costs of disasters.[35]

Meanwhile, nonmarket insurance mechanisms include those from the government (such as cash transfers, food and other in-kind transfers, and free primary health care); bilateral and multilateral aid resources; self-insurance such as dissaving; and informal support networks and mechanisms. Government support is especially useful in providing insurance during low-frequency and high-impact disasters, while community and informal mechanisms appear to work well in low-impact cases. All these mechanisms are, however, often insufficient at national, regional, and international levels (footnote 35). In developing economies around the world, more than 95% of disaster costs from weather- and climate-related hazards were not covered by insurance.[36] Thus, there is a strong need to bolster insurance mechanisms to diversify country risks from disasters across the developing world. Also, governments must undertake strategic approaches to leveraging and integrating new technologies and innovations such as real-time, high-frequency earth observation data into effective DRM and financing.[37]

C.   Preparing to Rebuild Better After a Disaster

Several challenges in disaster management occur in the aftermath of a disaster. Most pertain to problems relating to governance. Difficulties stem, for example, from overwhelmed local administrative capacity, or failure

[35]   Y. Sawada. 2017. Disasters, Household Decisions, and Insurance Mechanisms: A Review of Evidence and a Case Study from a Developing Country in Asia. *Asian Economic Policy Review*. 12 (1): pp. 18–40.

[36]   M. Golnaraghi, S. Surminski, and K. Schanz. 2016. *An Integrated Approach to Managing Extreme Events and Climate Risks. Towards a Concerted Public–Private Approach.* Zurich: The Geneva Association.

[37]   ADB and Organisation for Economic Co-operation and Development. 2020. *Leveraging Technology and Innovation for Disaster Risk Management and Financing.* Manila.

to consult with relevant local stakeholders, leading to delays in rebuilding. Addressing these challenges requires sound disaster risk strategies that include not just ways to fund recovery, but also to execute the budget and disburse funding swiftly and effectively.

Some challenges are long-term—when disaster reconstruction does little to reduce the risk of future disasters or when disasters have longer-lasting impacts on livelihoods and economic activities. Rebuilding for long-term recovery after a disaster is a complex process that requires close collaboration among national, subnational, and local governments. Often, however, authorities lack coordination and adequate capacity to plan and implement projects.[38]

Recognizing these problems, recent disaster management thinking has spawned new approaches to disaster recovery, rehabilitation, and reconstruction. The Sendai Framework was the first to officially emphasize the concept of rebuilding better or the idea that disaster recovery, rehabilitation, and reconstruction phases can be implemented such that nations and communities become more resilient than before a disaster struck. This can happen through "integrating disaster risk reduction measures into the restoration of physical infrastructure and societal systems, and into the revitalization of livelihoods, economies, and the environment."[39]

There is some evidence for external benefits of post-disaster reconstruction and recovery. These cases provide some support for Schumpeterian "creative destruction" in the context of disasters and post-disaster reconstruction. A noteworthy example is the May 2008 earthquake in Wenchuan county in the province of Sichuan, People's Republic of China (PRC). The earthquake, measuring 8.0 in the Richter scale, caused extensive damage, destroying property and critical infrastructure. Loss and damage were also recorded in the neighboring provinces of Gansu and Shaanxi. The cost of reconstruction was estimated at CNY1 trillion, nearly as large as Sichuan's gross provincial product. In 2009, the government allocated a quarter of its CNY4 trillion fiscal stimulus package in response to the global

---

[38] T. Lloyd-Jones. 2006. *Mind the Gap! Post-Disaster Reconstruction and the Transition from Humanitarian Relief.* London: Royal Institute of Chartered Surveyors.

[39] This definition is from the United Nations Intergovernmental Expert Working Group on Indicators and terminology, tasked with clarifying the central concepts that guide the Sendai Framework priorities.

financial crisis for earthquake reconstruction. In addition, a counterpart support plan was established by authorities, in which rich coastal areas were partnered with disaster-affected counties to assist in rebuilding by providing funding and mobilizing personnel and knowledge. The program resulted in more than 4,000 reconstruction projects and CNY91 billion in assistance for affected regions. In addition, the government provided large subsidies to affected households. Survey results conducted 10 months after the earthquake found that median income per person had climbed by 17.5%, while the poverty rate declined from 34% to 19% between 2007 and 2008.[40] The ensuing resurgence in the Sichuan economy lasted several years. This demonstrates how well-designed and well-implemented efforts from national and local governments have the potential to help disaster-affected areas in rebuilding better.

Dissecting the meaning of "rebuilding better," it is possible to summarize four objectives: safety, speed, fairness, and inclusivity. Safety—the avoidance of morbidity and mortality—is often the main guiding priority of post-disaster government policy. Safety can be achieved either through stronger and safety-equipped infrastructure or through softer approaches (such as planting mangroves before a storm or migrating out of disaster-prone areas). In one study on the elderly during the 2011 tsunami in Japan, it was found that those who have stronger social ties to the community were able to successfully evacuate in time.[41]

The speed of recovery is also important, through swift, efficient, and decisive implementation of well-designed post-disaster actions. However, there are usually several bottlenecks present, such as inadequate funding, lack of skilled personnel, legal impediments (such as unclear land tenure), or a sudden increase in construction costs. Speed can also run counter to other objectives of a "rebuilding better" policy, including the desire for safety or for inclusive consultation with the local community. But building back inclusively in ensuring a fair process and outcome is also crucial to achieving smooth recovery. Engaging the community through participatory planning and rebuilding consultations not only informs the design of DRM policies better, but will also yield stronger commitment to DRR and sustained recovery across the community. It is, therefore, unfortunate

---

[40] A. Park and S. Wang. 2017. Benefitting from Disaster? Public and Private Responses to the Wenchuan Earthquake. *World Development*. 94 (C): pp. 38–50.

[41] D. P. Aldrich and Y. Sawada. 2015. The Physical and Social Determinants of Mortality in the 3.11 Tsunami. *Social Science & Medicine* 124 (C): pp. 66–75.

that several studies find evidence that the most disadvantaged people in a society or community are often left out of the rebuilding process.[42]

Lastly, the process of rebuilding better should bring back economic potential to areas affected by disasters, or create sustainable employment and long-lasting income opportunities. Policy makers should design a reconstruction framework for this purpose, for without the prospects of jobs and continued livelihoods, recovery will be difficult or impossible.

---

[42] For example, refer to A. Karim and I. Noy. 2016. Poverty and Natural Disasters—A Qualitative Survey of the Empirical Literature. *Singapore Economic Review*. 61 (1): 1640001; S. Hallegate. 2014. *Natural Disasters and Climate Change: An Economic Perspective*. Berlin: Springer International Publishing; and Archana Patankar. 2019. Impacts of Natural Disasters on Households and Small Businesses in India. *ADB Economics Working Paper Series* No. 603. Manila: ADB (December).

PART 2:
THE COVID-19 DISASTER

Chapter V

COVID-19—
A GLOBAL HEALTH CRISIS

While individuals, businesses, and communities have persistently been exposed to a variety of natural hazards and human-made disasters,[43] the coronavirus disease (COVID-19) pandemic evolved into a global biological disaster that has proven to be one of the most serious, catastrophic events in human history.[44]

COVID-19 has spread to every continent. What started as a series of pneumonia cases of unknown cause in Wuhan Province, People's Republic of China (PRC), quickly morphed into a public health emergency worldwide. The disease spread rapidly within the PRC and beyond, surpassing the total number of cases and deaths from the severe acute respiratory syndrome (SARS) outbreak in 2003 and the Middle East respiratory syndrome (MERS) outbreak in 2012.[45] The pace and extent of transmission ultimately led the World Health Organization to declare the COVID-19 outbreak as a pandemic on 11 March 2020.

The number of cases continued to rise, both globally and within developing Asia. By 31 December 2020, COVID-19 had afflicted nearly 83.5 million people in 218 countries and territories, with a global death toll of more than 1.8 million. While the first case was reported in the PRC, by the end of 2020, the United States accounted for 24% of total cases (Figure 8, left panel). Developing Asia accounted for 17%, while Europe's share was 31%.

---

[43] Y. Sawada. 2007. The impact of natural and manmade disasters on household welfare. *Agricultural Economics*. 37 (s1): pp. 59–73.

[44] While COVID-19 was initially compared frequently with SARS and MERS, it has turned out to have much more substantial impact. Alternatively, the 1918–1920 Great Influenza Pandemic provides plausible upper bounds for outcomes under COVID-19 (R. J. Barro, J. F. Ursua, and J. Weng. 2020. The coronavirus and the great influenza pandemic: Lessons from the "Spanish flu" for the coronavirus's potential effects on mortality and economic activity. *NBER Working Paper* 26866. National Bureau of Economic Research. Cambridge, MA).

[45] For the economic analysis of SARS, refer to G. Wong. 2008. Has SARS infected the property market? Evidence from Hong Kong. *Journal of Urban Economics*. 63 (1): pp. 74–95; and N. Doan et al. 2020. The Economic Impacts of a Pandemic: What Happened after SARS in 2003? *CESifo Working Paper Series* 8687. Munich: Munich Society for the Promotion of Economic Research – CESifo GmbH.

Figure 8. Cumulative COVID-19 Cases Globally and in Developing Asia
(million, as of 31 December 2020)

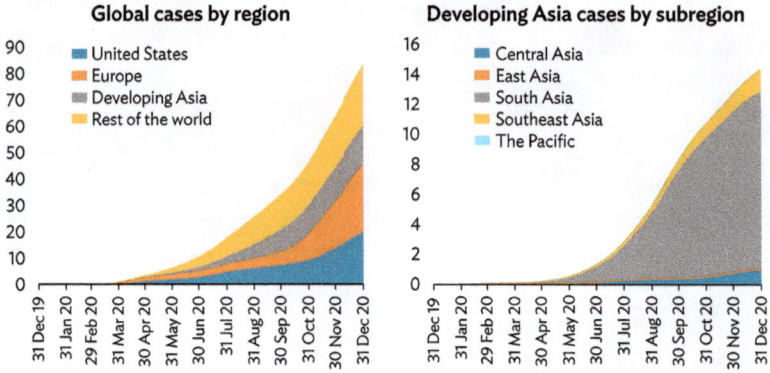

Source: M. Roser et al. 2021. *Coronavirus Pandemic (COVID-19)*. Published online at OurWorldInData.org. Retrieved on 18 January from https://ourworldindata.org/coronavirus.

Australia, Japan, and New Zealand collectively accounted for less than 0.5% of cases worldwide. Within developing Asia's 14.3 million infections, South Asia recorded the largest share, followed by Southeast Asia, Central Asia, East Asia, and the Pacific (Figure 8, right panel). In the fortnight ending 31 December 2020, daily new cases in the region remained high, reaching an average of more than 40,000. Of ADB's 46 members in developing Asia, 25 had domestic outbreaks of 1,000 cases or more.

Chapter VI
ECONOMIC IMPACT

The economic impact of the pandemic remains significant. ADB's December 2020 economic impact assessment estimated the extent of worldwide losses to be between $4.8 trillion and $7.4 trillion (or 5.5%–8.7% of global GDP) in 2020, and between $3.1 trillion and $5.4 trillion (3.6%–6.3% of global GDP) in 2021 (Table 2).[46] The same study also found that about 27%–30% of the global losses accrue to developing Asian economies, where the impact was estimated at $1.4 trillion–$2.2 trillion in 2020 (equivalent to 6.0%–9.5% of regional GDP), and $0.8 trillion–$1.5 trillion in 2021 (equivalent to 3.6%–6.3% of regional GDP). Compared to developing Asia, losses in the United States were slightly smaller in absolute terms and in terms of shares of GDP for both years. Meanwhile, estimated losses in Europe were larger than in developing Asia, both in absolute terms and as a share of GDP. By subregion, East Asian economies were expected to be hit less hard as they contained domestic outbreaks through aggressive testing and contact tracing, and avoided stringent lockdown measures and the associated sharp declines in mobility. The Pacific subregion also saw a somewhat smaller impact as no country had a significant outbreak and Papua New Guinea (the largest economy, which accounts for 68% of the subregion's GDP) was only minimally affected. However, this masked the large impact of COVID-19 on Pacific island economies that are heavily tourism-dependent; in many of these economies, the GDP loss from COVID-19 was in the double-digits.

Uncertainty surrounding the depth and duration of the COVID-19 pandemic dimmed economic prospects. In December 2020, ADB projected developing Asia as a whole would see an economic contraction of 0.4% in 2020[47]—a downward revision of more than 5 percentage points

---

[46] A. Abiad et al. 2020. The Impact of COVID-19 on Developing Asia: The Pandemic Extends into 2021. *ADB Brief* No. 159. Manila: ADB.

[47] ADB. 2020a. *Asian Development Outlook 2020 Supplement: Paths Diverge in Recovery from the Pandemic*. Manila (December).

Table 2. Estimated Global and Regional Losses Due to COVID-19
(relative to a no–COVID-19 baseline)

	2020					
	GDP (%)			GDP Loss ($ billion)		
	Better	Baseline	Worse	Better	Baseline	Worse
World	–5.5	–7.2	–8.7	4,757	6,165	7,441
Developing Asia	–6.0	–7.8	–9.5	1,394	1,818	2,211
Central Asia	–9.3	–11.9	–14.2	34	43	51
East Asia	–4.6	–6.0	–7.4	761	999	1,223
Southeast Asia	–8.6	–10.9	–12.7	253	320	374
South Asia	–10.0	–13.2	–16.3	343	453	560
The Pacific	–7.0	–8.7	–9.6	2	3	3
United States	–4.9	–6.4	–7.8	1,038	1,349	1,634
Europe	–7.9	–10.2	–12.2	1,488	1,913	2,285
Rest of the world	–3.6	–4.6	–5.6	836	1,084	1,310

	2021					
	GDP (%)			GDP Loss ($ billion)		
	Better	Baseline	Worse	Better	Baseline	Worse
World	–3.6	–4.9	–6.3	3,108	4,234	5,407
Developing Asia	–3.6	–4.9	–6.3	844	1,148	1,470
Central Asia	–6.2	–8.6	–11.1	23	31	40
East Asia	–2.4	–3.3	–4.2	402	547	698
Southeast Asia	–6.1	–8.4	–11.0	178	246	322
South Asia	–7.0	–9.4	–11.8	240	322	406
The Pacific	–3.8	–5.6	–7.8	1	2	3
United States	–3.3	–4.5	–5.8	696	947	1,212
Europe	–5.1	–7.0	–9.0	956	1,311	1,697
Rest of the world	–2.6	–3.5	–4.4	612	828	1,027

GDP = gross domestic product.

Source: A. Abiad et al. 2020. The Impact of COVID-19 on Developing Asia: The Pandemic Extends into 2021. *ADB Brief* No. 159. Manila: Asian Development Bank.

relative to pre-COVID-19 forecasts,[48] and its worst economic performance in 6 decades; a V-shaped recovery of real GDP was unlikely.[49] Figure 9 offers a visual representation of the updated forecasts, and how they had been revised relative to the pre-COVID-19 forecasts in December 2019. No economy escaped the negative economic impact from COVID-19, with all forecasts being revised downward (the vertical axis). Contractions were expected in 31 of 46 ADB members; the rest were expected to grow at very low rates (the horizontal axis). The process of normalizing economic activity will be hampered by continued social distancing and possible new outbreaks. And even if individual economies succeed in normalizing domestic activity, they will be held back by a very weak external environment and potentially disrupted supply chains.

The outbreak affected economies through numerous channels. These included (i) sharp declines in domestic consumption in outbreak-affected economies as people's mobility was restrained, resulting in severe declines in business sales as well as in investment spending—as the outbreak prompted less optimistic sentiment on future business activity; (ii) declines, and sometimes even cessation, of tourism and business travel because of border closures; (iii) spillovers of weaker demand onto other sectors and economies through trade and production linkages; and (iv) supply-side disruptions to production and trade distinct from demand-side shocks spilling over through trade and production linkages. For example, measures to contain COVID-19 undercut developing Asia's domestic demand. Figure 10 shows the diversity in experience of selected regional members in the number of cases, stringency of control measures, and mobility changes. While a general trade-off is observed between health outcome (captured by the containment index in the blue line) and economic level (captured by the mobility level in the orange line), it is not necessarily unavoidable. As can be seen, countries such as the Republic of Korea wisely avoided this trade-off by adopting smart lockdown policies through strict (digital-based) testing and contact tracing.[50]

With people staying at home, private consumption dropped sharply. Travel and tourism was particularly hard-hit. The domestic and external

---

[48] ADB. 2019b. *Asian Development Outlook 2019 Supplement: Growth Slows Further in Developing Asia's Giants.* Manila (December projected 2020 growth at 5.2%).

[49] ADB. 2020a. *Asian Development Outlook 2020 Supplement: Paths Diverge in Recovery from the Pandemic.* Manila (December).

[50] ADB. 2020b. *Asian Development Outlook 2020 Update: Wellness in Worrying Times.* Manila.

Figure 9. Latest Forecasts versus Pre-COVID-19 Forecasts, 2020

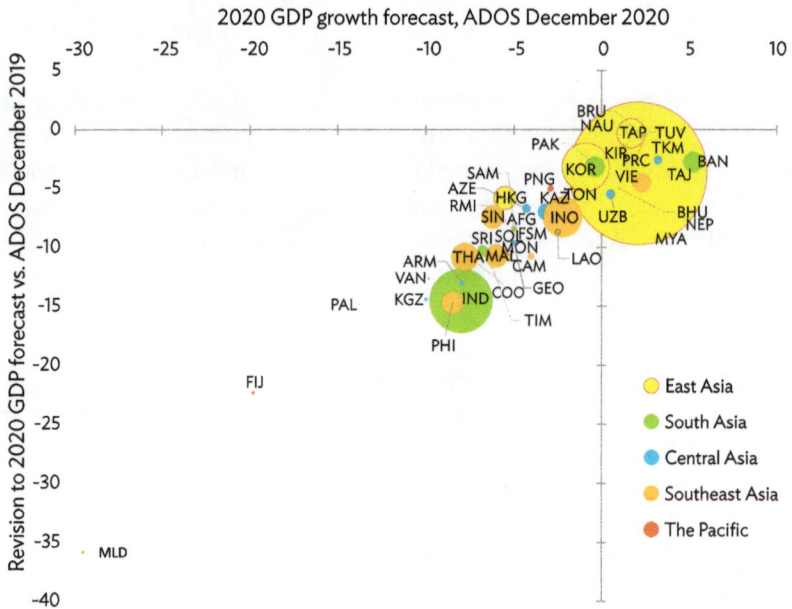

2020 GDP growth forecast, ADOS December 2020

Legend:
- East Asia
- South Asia
- Central Asia
- Southeast Asia
- The Pacific

ADO = Asian Development Outlook; ADOS = ADO Supplement; AFG = Afghanistan; ARM = Armenia; AZE = Azerbaijan; BAN = Bangladesh; BHU = Bhutan; BRU = Brunei Darussalam; CAM = Cambodia; COO = Cook Islands; FIJ = Fiji; FSM = Federated States of Micronesia; GDP = gross domestic product; GEO = Georgia; HKG = Hong Kong, China; IND = India; INO = Indonesia; KAZ = Kazakhstan; KGZ = Kyrgyz Republic; KIR = Kiribati; KOR = Republic of Korea; LAO = Lao People's Democratic Republic; MAL = Malaysia; MLD = Maldives; MON = Mongolia; MYA = Myanmar; NAU = Nauru; NEP = Nepal; PAK = Pakistan; PAL = Palau; PHI = Philippines; PNG = Papua New Guinea; PRC = People's Republic of China; RMI = Marshall Islands; SAM = Samoa; SIN = Singapore; SOL = Solomon Islands; SRI = Sri Lanka; TAJ = Tajikistan; TAP = Taipei,China; THA = Thailand; TIM = Timor-Leste; TKM = Turkmenistan; TON = Tonga; TUV = Tuvalu; UZB = Uzbekistan; VAN = Vanuatu; VIE = Viet Nam.

Note: Bubble size indicates the value of 2019 nominal GDP.

Sources: Asian Development Bank. 2019b. *Asian Development Outlook 2019 Supplement: Growth Slows Further in Developing Asia's Giants*. Manila (December); and Asian Development Bank. 2020a. *Asian Development Outlook 2020 Supplement: Paths Diverge in Recovery from the Pandemic*. Manila (December).

Figure 10. COVID-19 Cases, Stringency of Control, and Mobility for Selected Economies

India

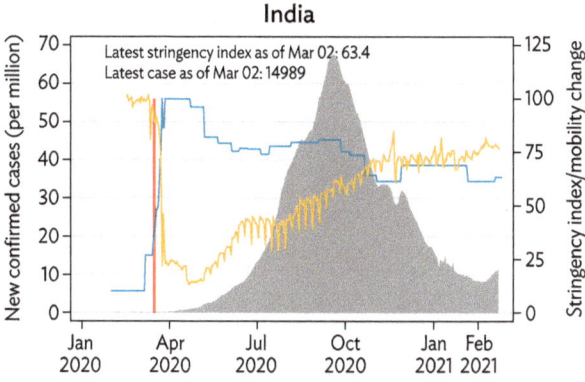

Latest stringency index as of Mar 02: 63.4
Latest case as of Mar 02: 14989

Indonesia

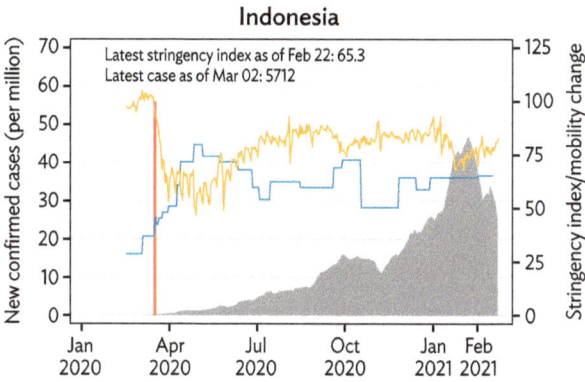

Latest stringency index as of Feb 22: 65.3
Latest case as of Mar 02: 5712

Republic of Korea

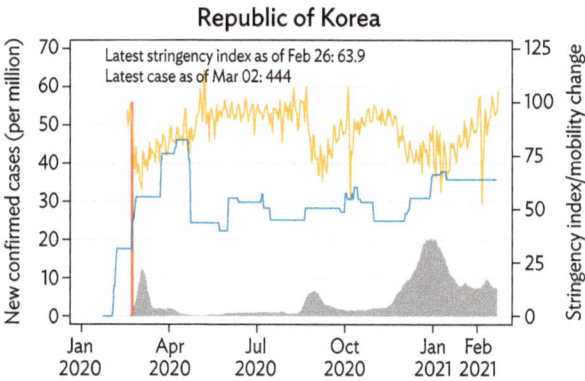

Latest stringency index as of Feb 26: 63.9
Latest case as of Mar 02: 444

▨ New confirmed cases (7-day moving average)   — Stringency index
▬ Total confirmed cases reach at least 100   — Mobility change (retail and recreation)

continued on next page

Figure 10 *continued*

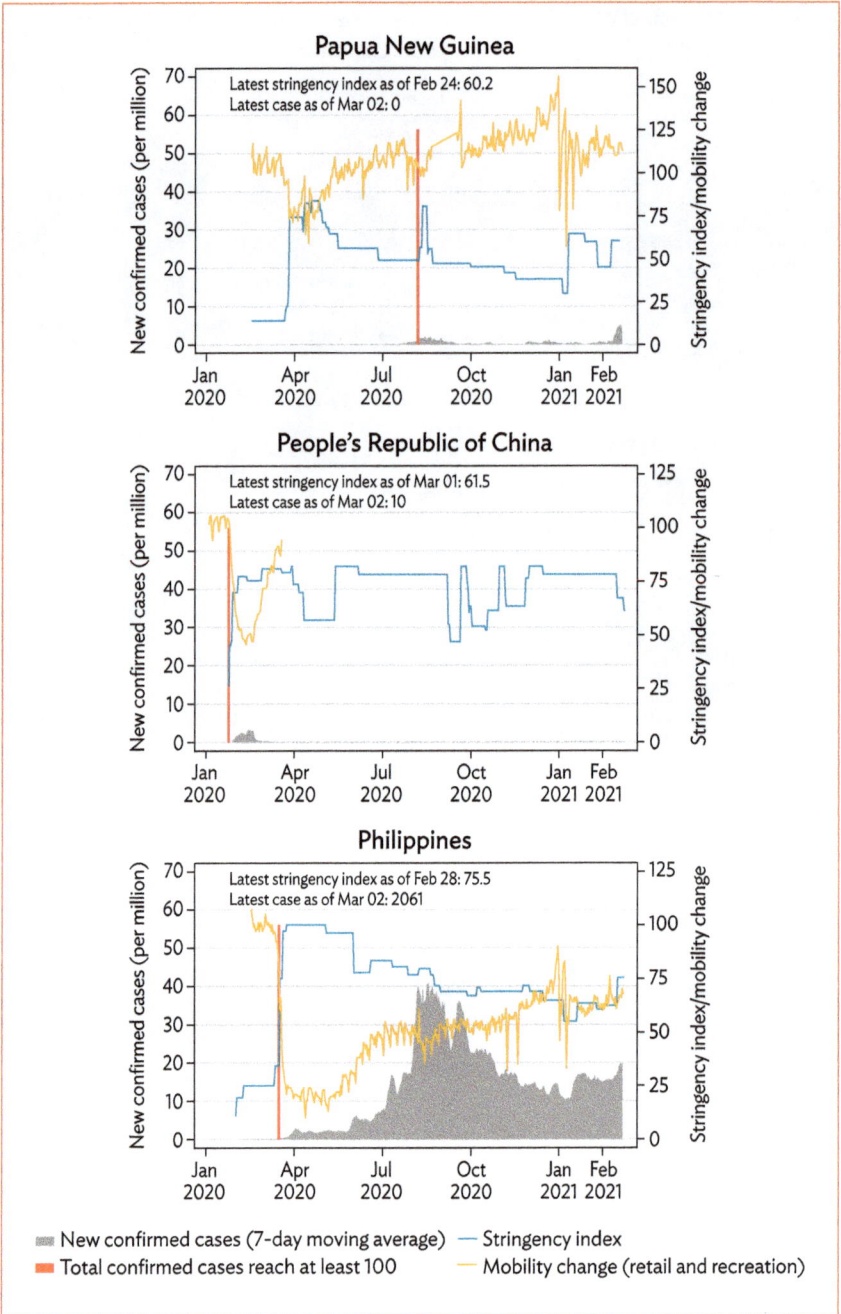

Papua New Guinea

Latest stringency index as of Feb 24: 60.2
Latest case as of Mar 02: 0

People's Republic of China

Latest stringency index as of Mar 01: 61.5
Latest case as of Mar 02: 10

Philippines

Latest stringency index as of Feb 28: 75.5
Latest case as of Mar 02: 2061

New confirmed cases (7-day moving average) — Stringency index
Total confirmed cases reach at least 100 — Mobility change (retail and recreation)

continued on next page

Figure 10 *continued*

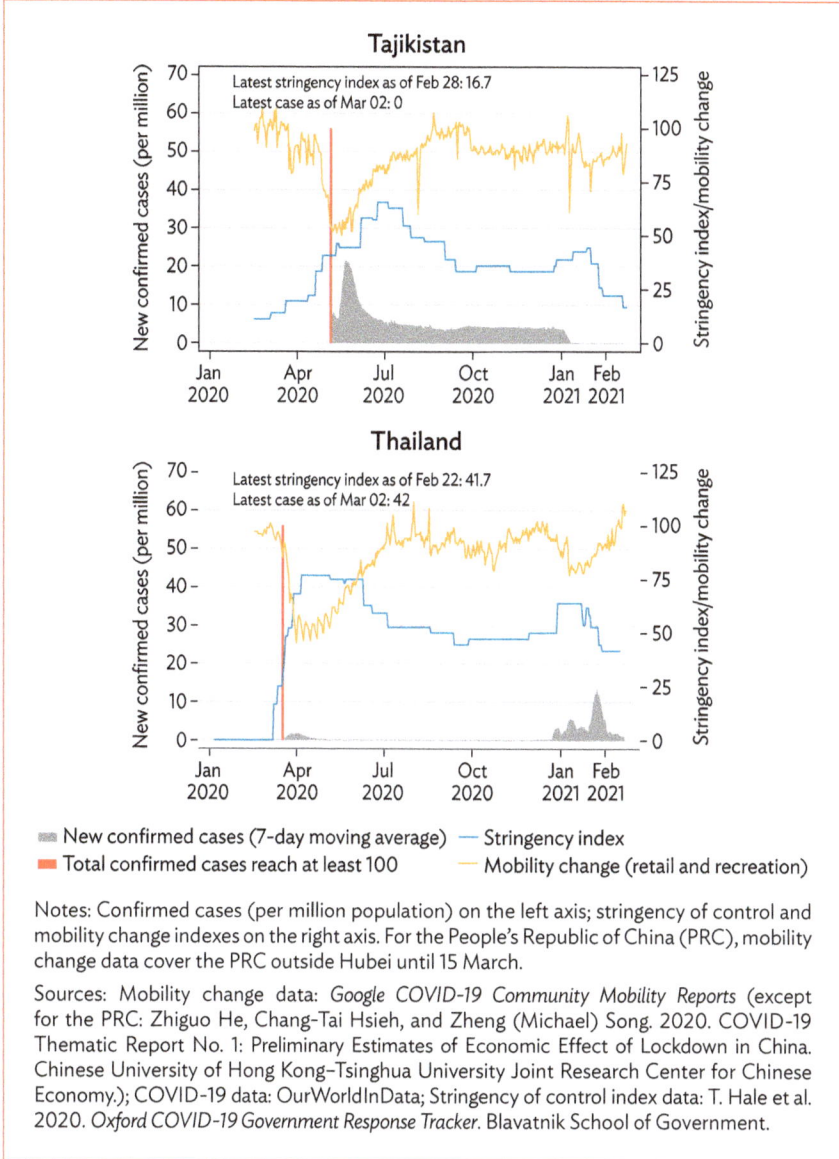

Tajikistan

Latest stringency index as of Feb 28: 16.7
Latest case as of Mar 02: 0

Thailand

Latest stringency index as of Feb 22: 41.7
Latest case as of Mar 02: 42

▬ New confirmed cases (7-day moving average) — Stringency index
▬ Total confirmed cases reach at least 100 — Mobility change (retail and recreation)

Notes: Confirmed cases (per million population) on the left axis; stringency of control and mobility change indexes on the right axis. For the People's Republic of China (PRC), mobility change data cover the PRC outside Hubei until 15 March.

Sources: Mobility change data: *Google COVID-19 Community Mobility Reports* (except for the PRC: Zhiguo He, Chang-Tai Hsieh, and Zheng (Michael) Song. 2020. COVID-19 Thematic Report No. 1: Preliminary Estimates of Economic Effect of Lockdown in China. Chinese University of Hong Kong–Tsinghua University Joint Research Center for Chinese Economy.); COVID-19 data: OurWorldInData; Stringency of control index data: T. Hale et al. 2020. *Oxford COVID-19 Government Response Tracker*. Blavatnik School of Government.

demand shocks spilled over to other sectors and economies through trade and production linkages. Supply-side disruptions reverberated across developing Asia. Figure 11 presents the pandemic impact on five subregions, plus an additional group on small tourism-dependent economies with three impact components—domestic demand decline (blue), international

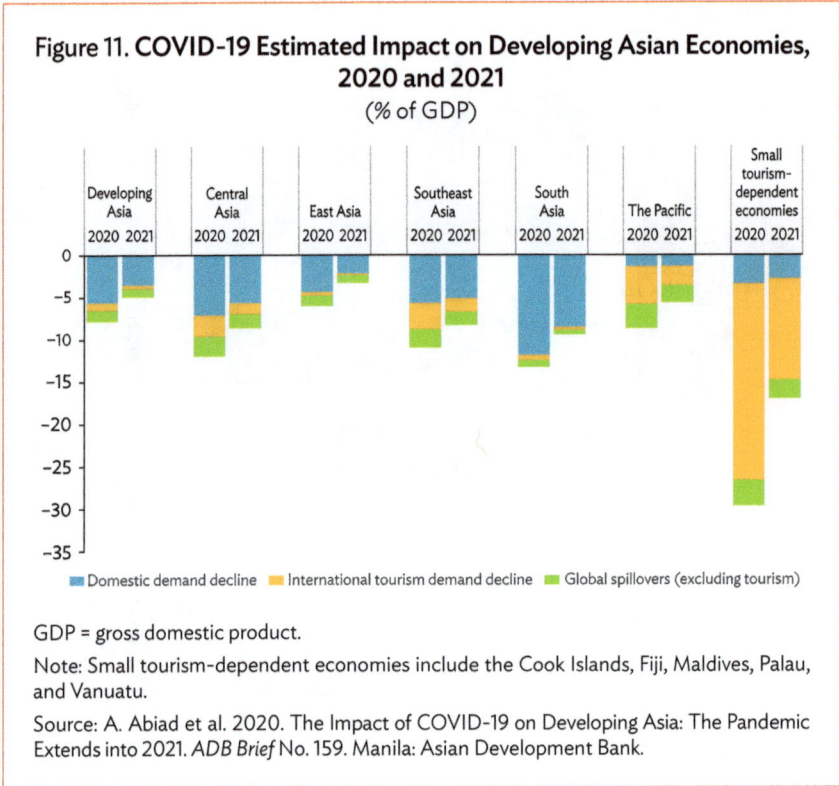

Figure 11. COVID-19 Estimated Impact on Developing Asian Economies, 2020 and 2021
(% of GDP)

GDP = gross domestic product.

Note: Small tourism-dependent economies include the Cook Islands, Fiji, Maldives, Palau, and Vanuatu.

Source: A. Abiad et al. 2020. The Impact of COVID-19 on Developing Asia: The Pandemic Extends into 2021. *ADB Brief* No. 159. Manila: Asian Development Bank.

tourism decline (orange), and global spillovers excluding tourism (green). The largest impacts were in South Asia and in the small tourism-dependent economies because of a sharp decline in domestic demand and tourism, respectively. In 2021, the pattern of losses remains the same, although amounts are smaller.

The pandemic has severely strained firms, especially micro, small, and medium-sized enterprises. Many suspended operations after the virus outbreak and were compelled to reduce their workforce because of poor domestic demand as a result of strict lockdown measures, leaving them with sharply reduced sales and revenue.[51]

---

[51] S. Shinozaki. 2020. The COVID-19 Impact on Micro, Small, and Medium-Sized Enterprises: Evidence from Rapid Surveys in Indonesia, the Lao People's Democratic Republic, the Philippines, and Thailand. In B. Susantono, Y. Sawada, and C.Y. Park (eds). *Navigating COVID-19 in Asia and the Pacific*. Manila: ADB; and ADB. 2020c. *Asia Small and Medium-Sized Enterprise Monitor 2020 – Volume II: COVID-19 Impact on Micro, Small and Medium-Sized Enterprises in Developing Asia*. Manila.

The pandemic put many jobs at risk, with some jobs lost permanently. Unskilled workers, women, informal sector workers, and foreign migrant workers were heavily affected. Workers in the informal sector were particularly hard-hit, as they receive low wages and lack access to social protection. Even before the pandemic, technological change was leading to a polarization of low- and high-skilled jobs and a hollowing out of middle-skilled jobs; the virus impact accelerated the digital transformation and job polarization, widening wage inequality.[52] Thus, the pandemic could worsen overall income inequality.

Jobs held by migrant workers became particularly vulnerable, potentially undercutting remittances. Severe migrant job losses were reported in retail trade, manufacturing, hospitality and recreation, and accommodation and food service sectors. In addition, border control restrictions put migrant worker job security and well-being in peril. Crucial remittances sent to their families are expected to decline dramatically. It is estimated that total remittances to developing Asia fell by between $31.0 billion and $53.5 billion in 2020, or a drop in remittance value of from 11.6% to 20.0%.[53] This is especially difficult for economies heavily reliant on remittances, such as Tonga, Tajikistan, the Kyrgyz Republic, and Nepal, where remittance receipts account for at least a quarter of GDP. With many households in developing Asia dependent on international remittances—particularly in the Pacific and Central and West Asia—a sudden stop in remittance flows could push people into poverty.

The crisis could thus reverse years of progress toward eliminating poverty in developing Asia. Before the pandemic, the region was on a path of continued steady reduction in poverty rates and in the number of poor. Had the trajectory been in line with 2012–2018 data, there would have been an estimated 734 million (or about 19%) living in poverty as defined by the $3.20 per day international poverty line in 2020, and an estimated 114 million (or about 3%) living in extreme poverty as defined by the $1.90 per day international poverty line (Figure 12). However, as mentioned, the pandemic adversely affected livelihoods, cutting into economic activity, earnings, remittances, and consumption. In 2020, COVID-19 is projected to add 162 million and 78 million to the poor in developing Asia in terms of

---

[52] C.Y. Park and A. M. Inocencio. 2020. COVID-19, Technology, and Polarizing Jobs. *ADB Brief* No. 147. Manila: ADB.

[53] A. Takenaka et al. 2020. COVID-19 Impact on International Migration, Remittances, and Recipient Households in Developing Asia. *ADB Brief* No. 148. Manila: ADB.

Figure 12. **Simulated Poverty Impact in Developing Asia**
(number of poor in millions)

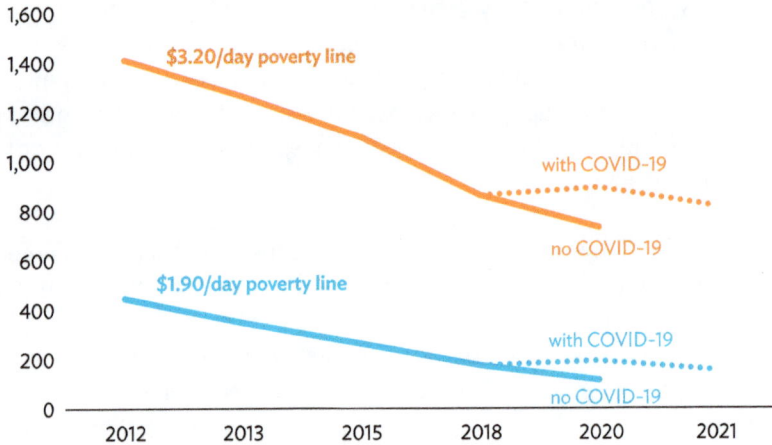

COVID-19 = coronavirus disease.

Notes: Developing Asia refers to the average of 34 Asian Development Bank (ADB) developing member countries. For 2018, India's estimates were based on extrapolations using the World Bank's model-based mean per capita expenditure in 2015, gross domestic product per capita growth rates between 2015 and 2018, and distribution based on the 2011–2012 household consumption survey.

Source: J. Bulan et al. 2020. COVID-19 and Poverty: Some Scenarios. Manila (unpublished note prepared for the Economic Research and Regional Cooperation Department, ADB).

the $3.20 per day and $1.90 per day international poverty lines, respectively. By 2021, as the region's economy rebounds, poverty is expected to return closer to its pre-COVID-19 level.[54]

On the financial front, risks of financial turmoil and financial crises cannot be discounted. In the early stages of the pandemic, especially in March and April 2020, movements in equity markets, exchange rates, bond spreads, and volatility indexes had been sharp, reminiscent of the global financial crisis of 2008–2009 (and in some cases exceeding it). However, markets stabilized after the turmoil's peak in March and April 2020. Evidence suggests that heightened financial volatility and a sudden stop in capital flows to the region are distinct possibilities. Particularly, the projected contraction in majority of developing Asia's economies raised concerns

---

[54] J. Bulan et al. 2020. COVID-19 and Poverty: Some Scenarios. Manila (unpublished note prepared for the Economic Research and Regional Cooperation Department, ADB).

about the threat of rising nonperforming loans (NPLs) and financial instability. The pandemic-induced slowdown implies lower corporate earnings and higher unemployment, exacerbating the debt service burden for both firms and households. Many corporations, especially micro, small, and medium-sized enterprises, face the risk of default because of prolonged forced business closures. Job losses also imply rising household debt and mortgage defaults. Lenders are bound to suffer from loan losses and rising NPLs. Emerging market economies could be vulnerable to a withdrawal of funds by major global lenders as NPLs rise.[55]

---

[55] C. Y. Park and K. Shin. 2020. The Impact of Nonperforming Loans on Cross-Border Bank Lending: Implications for Emerging Market Economies. *ADB Brief* No. 136. Manila: ADB.

Chapter VII

GOVERNMENT RESPONSES

Governments worldwide took steps to mitigate the economic impact. At the same time that authorities around the world adopted containment measures that restricted mobility and economic activity, many announced massive support packages to help households and businesses cope with the economic shock. By 11 January 2021, according to data from the ADB COVID-19 Policy Database, ADB members had announced policy packages totaling $27.1 trillion, the heftiest of which was from the United States at $8.1 trillion.[56] The amount announced by developing Asian economies was $3.6 trillion, accounting for 15.2% of regional GDP (Figure 13). More than half was focused on providing direct income support to mitigate the damage to households and firms. Interventions to reinforce money markets and credit creation were also important in avoiding a credit crisis. It is noteworthy that there is a distinct possibility that actual disbursements will not match announced package amounts. The extent of these policy packages was also uneven across developing Asia.

COVID-19 responses strained government fiscal positions. Sharply slower economic growth and fiscal policy responses raised public debt ratios. The pandemic severely deteriorated short-term growth forecasts for many countries in the region. A drop in fiscal revenue, coupled with unplanned spending and countercyclical policies used to stem the crisis, caused primary deficits to widen dramatically. Economies that used to be associated with a favorable combination of low debt (below 50% of GDP) and fiscal surpluses were pushed into situations characterized by high debt (above 50% of GDP) and fiscal deficits.[57] From *ADO Supplement – December 2020* growth projections for 2020 and 2021, the average public debt ratio among developing member countries was projected to rise to 50.9% of

---

[56] J. Felipe and S. Fullwiler 2020. ADB COVID-19 Policy Database: A Guide. *Asian Development Review* 37(2): pp. 1–20.

[57] B. Ferrarini et al. Forthcoming. Asia Sovereign Debt Monitor. Manila: ADB.

Figure 13. Packages Announced in Developing Asia by Subregion and Policy Measure
(% of GDP)

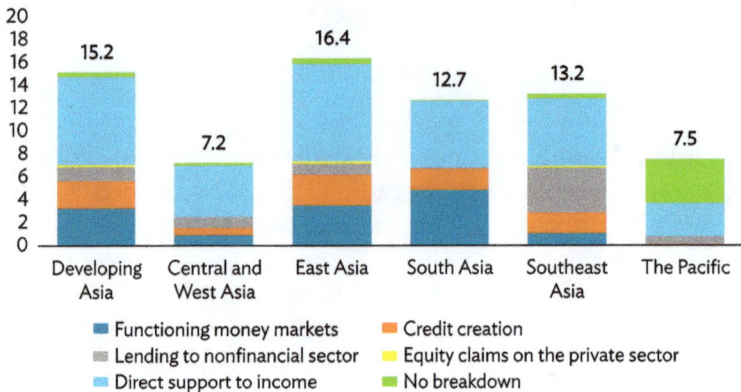

GDP = gross domestic product.

Notes: Data as of 11 January 2021.

Sources: ADB COVID-19 Policy Database (accessed 16 January 2021). For the database, refer to J. Felipe and S. Fullwiler. 2020. ADB COVID-19 Policy Database: A Guide. *Asian Development Review* 37(2): pp. 1–20.

Box 2. ADB's Response to the COVID-19 Crisis

The Asian Development Bank (ADB) is supporting its developing member countries' pandemic responses with finance, knowledge, and partnerships. ADB announced a $20 billion package of quick-disbursing loans, grants, and technical assistance, plus approved measures to streamline its operations for quicker and more flexible assistance delivery. ADB provides support via its countercyclical support programs (including the newly established COVID-19 Pandemic Response Option [CPRO]), emergency assistance loans, and other instruments, if needed. In 2020, ADB financing commitments for coronavirus disease (COVID-19) response projects amounted to $16.1 billion. This included 26 CPROs; other sovereign projects; nonsovereign projects and programs; technical assistance projects; and projects under the trade finance, supply chain finance, and microfinance programs (Box Table). In addition, $10.8 billion in cofinancing was committed for these projects. On the knowledge front, ADB conducted numerous economic impact assessments and analyses of the pandemic and its effects. It also convened partnerships

continued on next page

Box 2 *continued*

with other international organizations and the broader global community as part of ADB's overall response strategy. For vaccines, ADB launched a $9 billion vaccine facility, the Asia Pacific Vaccine Access Facility in December 2020, to support its low- and middle-income members procure and deliver COVID-19 vaccines.

Box Table. Summary of ADB's Commitments[a] in Support of Developing Member Countries' COVID-19 Response, 2020
($ million)

Item	ADB	Cofinancing	Total
Sovereign operations	13,280	8,187	21,467
Nonsovereign operations	448	158	606
Trade Finance, Supply Chain Finance, and Microfinance Programs[b]	2,419	2,496	4,915
Total	**16,147**	**10,841**	**26,988**

ADB = Asian Development Bank, COVID-19 = coronavirus disease.

[a] Commitment is the financing approved by the ADB Board of Directors or Management for which the legal agreement has been signed by the borrower, recipient, or the investee company and ADB. It is the amount indicated in the investment agreement that may or may not be equal to the approved amount, depending on the exchange rate at the time of signing. In the case of official and commercial cofinancing not administered by ADB for which the signed amount is not readily available, the approved amount is used.

[b] The Trade Finance Program represents 92% of the ADB figure and supported 7,178 transactions in the reporting period, with an average maturity of 159 days.

Source: Extracted from Asian Development Bank. 2021. Annual Report 2020. Manila.

GDP by 2021, a significant increase from 42.5% of GDP in 2019.[58] Figure 14 shows the public debt ratios for 44 ADB regional members with available data using ADB's debt projection model. Projected increases in public debt ratios between 2019 and 2021 were largest for Bhutan, Maldives, and Fiji, exceeding 20 percentage points for each.

---

[58] These figures are simple unweighted averages across 44 ADB regional members for which projections are available, hiding much variation among economies.

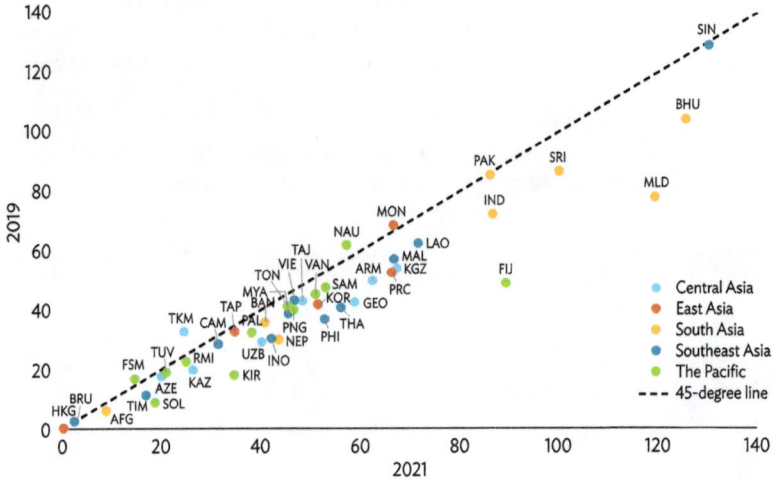

Figure 14. **Public Debt**
(% of GDP)

AFG = Afghanistan; ARM = Armenia; AZE = Azerbaijan; BAN = Bangladesh; BHU = Bhutan; BRU = Brunei Darussalam; CAM = Cambodia; FIJ = Fiji; FSM = Federated States of Micronesia; GDP = gross domestic product; GEO = Georgia; HKG = Hong Kong, China; IND = India; INO = Indonesia; KAZ = Kazakhstan; KGZ = Kyrgyz Republic; KIR = Kiribati; KOR = Republic of Korea; LAO = Lao People's Democratic Republic; MAL = Malaysia; MLD = Maldives; MON = Mongolia; MYA = Myanmar; NAU = Nauru; NEP = Nepal; PAK = Pakistan; PAL = Palau; PHI = Philippines; PNG = Papua New Guinea; PRC = People's Republic of China; RMI = Marshall Islands; SAM = Samoa; SIN = Singapore; SOL = Solomon Islands; SRI = Sri Lanka; TAJ = Tajikistan; TAP = Taipei,China; THA = Thailand; TIM = Timor-Leste; TKM = Turkmenistan; TON = Tonga; TUV = Tuvalu; UZB = Uzbekistan; VAN = Vanuatu; VIE = Viet Nam.

Source: B. Ferrarini et al. Forthcoming. Asia Sovereign Debt Monitor. Manila: Asian Development Bank.

Chapter VIII

LOOKING AHEAD

In the future, natural hazards will remain a tremendous threat to the gains that developing Asia's economies have worked so hard to achieve over the past half century. Effective policies for disaster resilience are, therefore, needed to mitigate both short- and long-term effects of disasters. When pervasive, disasters can permeate across time and locations, hitting the region's poorest households, communities, or entire economies. Indeed, the COVID-19 pandemic demonstrated that disasters can cross borders, persist over prolonged periods, and strike the most vulnerable. This experience underscores the importance of disaster preparedness, swift responsiveness, and sustainable recovery.

Over the past 50 years, developing Asia achieved much progress in designing and implementing strategies to reduce the risks from natural hazards. Yet, no one was ready for COVID-19. Several challenges remain.

First, the region spends more on disaster response than on disaster reduction and resilience. Higher spending on disaster prevention and preparedness (instead of disaster response) can potentially provide multiple development benefits, even in normal times (for example, tsunami or cyclone shelters can be used as classrooms or community centers). This preparedness must cover all forms of potential disasters, including biological ones like COVID-19.

Second, carefully planning, designing, and investing in climate-resilient and disaster-resilient infrastructure dramatically reduce the exposure and vulnerability to various types of disaster risk (from both frequent and rare events). For example, planning also involves choosing the right locations and avoiding building infrastructure in risky and disaster-prone areas—decreasing exposure to hazards substantially. It also means having sufficient hard and soft infrastructure, including health-care workers and facilities, to address calamities.

Third, insurance mechanisms in developing Asia need to be more broadly available and accessible. Since 1980, more than 90% of all catastrophic losses have been uninsured. Policies that bolster market and nonmarket insurance mechanisms will dramatically cut losses across households (especially after catastrophic disasters). Recent innovative insurance models are promising (such as index-based risk-transfer instruments). Reinsurance, meanwhile, distributes risk more widely, helping governments provide safety nets to vulnerable populations. Related to this, stronger social protection programs—in terms of expanded coverage and greater delivery efficiency—can help ease the harmful impact on the poor and vulnerable. In addition, public policy should limit the unemployment impact on workers and their families by providing disaster victims temporary income support (such as unemployment insurance systems, redundancy payments, and social assistance programs) and by employing active labor market policies (such as labor exchanges or mobility assistance, education and training, and business support or subsidized employment).[59]

Fourth, it is critically important to engage the community in planning for disaster reduction, response, and recovery. Community action, as first response to disasters, should complement national efforts. Community resilience can become an essential part of a nation's consciousness through training and education. Recent experience in Asia also shows how communities and local knowledge help timely evacuation and effective delivery of humanitarian and recovery assistance. During the COVID-19 pandemic, informed community leaders helped stem contagion and allowed for the tracing of local residents who had been in contact with those infected.

Fifth, comprehensive planning and strategies for reconstruction—"rebuilding better"—stress safety, timeliness, inclusion, climate resilience, and the full realization of economic potential. Preparing for rebuilding better requires planning for a sustainable recovery, bridging the gap between the short-term humanitarian response and long-term rebuilding and reconstruction. For example, COVID-19 responses must be forged to address longer-term challenges by focusing on resilient, green infrastructure investments that can help jump-start economies, while moving them down a more environmentally sustainable path. Greening the post-pandemic recovery can spur industry, create jobs, and help build resilience against

---

[59] B. Susantono, Y. Sawada, and C. Y. Park. 2020. Navigating COVID-19 in Asia and the Pacific. Manila: ADB.

future hazards.[60] Effective governance is crucial, as well as clarity of the roles and responsibilities that all stakeholders play. Boosting skills and absorptive capacity is critical to quickly and effectively manage the influx of resources during the immediate aftermath of disasters.

Finally, disaster recovery should apply new technologies and innovations to be inclusive and equitable across all segments of society, particularly the most vulnerable and disadvantaged. For example, the COVID-19 pandemic has substantially affected all sectors, with a disproportionate impact on the poor and vulnerable, along with the services sector. An accelerated digital transformation can help micro, small, and medium-sized enterprises access supply chains and enhance consumer welfare. Investing in digital readiness and developing the required skills for the digital economy can help mitigate the impact of post–COVID-19 pandemic structural changes in both work and workplace. Governments should ensure that there is adequate investment in high-speed broadband and fiber networks, while designing appropriate regulatory regimes with proper incentives and governance mechanisms. They should invest in skills development for those unemployed and furloughed because of disasters, as well as those of the future workforce (footnote 51).[61]

---

[60] A. Mehta and N. C. Morgado. 2020. Build green to help fend off the next pandemic. *Asian Development Blog*. 6 May.

[61] C.Y. Park and A. M. Inocencio. 2020. COVID-19, Technology, and Polarizing Jobs. *ADB Brief* No. 147. Manila: ADB.

REFERENCES

Abiad, Abdul, Reizle Platitas, Jesson Pagaduan, Christian Regle Jabagat, and Editha Laviña. 2020. The Impact of COVID-19 on Developing Asia: The Pandemic Extends into 2021. *ADB Brief* No. 159. Manila: Asian Development Bank (ADB).

ADB COVID-19 Policy Database (accessed 16 January 2021).

Aldrich, Daniel P., and Yasuyuki Sawada. 2015. The Physical and Social Determinants of Mortality in the 3.11 Tsunami. *Social Science & Medicine* 124 (C): pp. 66–75.

Asian Development Bank (ADB). 2016. *Disaster Risk in Asia and the Pacific: Assessment, Management, and Finance.* Manila.

ADB. 2017. *Meeting Asia's Infrastructure Needs.* Manila.

ADB. 2019a. *Asian Development Outlook 2019: Strengthening Disaster Resilience.* Manila.

ADB. 2019b. *Asian Development Outlook 2019 Supplement: Growth Slows Further in Developing Asia's Giants.* Manila (December).

ADB. 2020a. *Asian Development Outlook 2020 Supplement: Paths Diverge in Recovery from the Pandemic.* Manila (December).

ADB. 2020b. *Asian Development Outlook 2020 Update: Wellness in Worrying Times.* Manila.

ADB. 2020c. *Asia Small and Medium-Sized Enterprise Monitor 2020 – Volume II: COVID-19 Impact on Micro, Small and Medium-Sized Enterprises in Developing Asia.* Manila.

ADB. 2021. *Annual Report 2020.* Manila.

ADB and Organisation for Economic Co-operation and Development. 2020. *Leveraging Technology and Innovation for Disaster Risk Management and Financing.* Manila.

Barro, Robert J., Jose F. Ursua, and Joanna Weng. 2020. The coronavirus and the great influenza pandemic: Lessons from the "Spanish flu" for the coronavirus's potential effects on mortality and economic activity. *NBER Working Paper* 26866. Cambridge, Massachusetts: National Bureau of Economic Research.

Bulan, Joseph, Rana Hasan, Arturo Martinez, and Iva Sebastian. 2020. COVID-19 and Poverty: Some Scenarios. Manila (unpublished note prepared for the Economic Research and Regional Cooperation Department, ADB).

Caruso, German and Sebastian Miller. 2015. Long Run Effects and Intergenerational Transmission of Natural Disasters: A Case Study on the 1970 Ancash Earthquake. *Journal of Development Economics.* 117 (C): pp. 134–150.

Carvalho, Vasco M., Makoto Nirei, Yukiko U. Saito, and Alireza Tahbaz-Salehi. 2021. Supply Chain Disruptions: Evidence from the Great East Japan Earthquake. *Quarterly Journal of Economics.* 136 (2): pp. 1255–1321.

Cas, Ava Gail, Elizabeth Frankenberg, Wayan Suriastini, and Duncan Thomas. 2014. The Impact of Parental Death on Child Well-being: Evidence from the Indian Ocean Tsunami. *Demography.* 51 (2): pp. 437–457.

Davis, Donald R. and David E. Weinstein. 2002. Bones, Bombs, and Break Points: The Geography of Economic Activity. *American Economic Review.* 92 (5): pp. 1269–1289.

Doan, Nguyen, Canh Phuc Nguyen, Ilan Noy, and Yasuyuki Sawada. 2020. The Economic Impacts of a Pandemic: What Happened after SARS in 2003? *CESifo Working Paper Series* 8687. Munich: Munich Society for the Promotion of Economic Research – CESifo GmbH.

duPont, William IV, Ilan Noy, Yoko Okuyama, and Yasuyuki Sawada. 2015. The Long-Run Socio-Economic Consequences of a Disaster: The 1995 Earthquake in Kobe. *PLoS ONE.* 10 (10): e0138714.

EM-DAT: The Emergency Events Database - Université Catholique de Louvain (UCL) - CRED, D. Guha-Sapir - www.emdat.be (accessed 25 January 2021), Brussels, Belgium.

Felipe, Jesus and Scott Fullwiler. 2020. ADB COVID-19 Policy Database: A Guide. *Asian Development Review* 37(2): pp. 1–20.

Ferrarini, Benno, Juan Jose Pradelli, Paul Mariano, and Suzette Dagli. Forthcoming. Asia Sovereign Debt Monitor. Manila: ADB.

Golnaraghi, Maryam, Swenja Surminski, and Kai-Uwe Schanz. 2016. *An Integrated Approach to Managing Extreme Events and Climate Risks. Towards a Concerted Public–Private Approach*. Zurich: The Geneva Association.

Google COVID-19 Community Mobility Reports.

Government of Japan, Cabinet Office. 2015. *Disaster Management in Japan*. Tokyo.

Hale, Thomas, Noam Angrist, Emily Cameron-Blake, Laura Hallas, Beatriz Kira, Saptarshi Majumdar, Anna Petherick, Toby Phillips, Helen Tatlow, and Samuel Webster. 2020. Oxford COVID-19 Government Response Tracker. Blavatnik School of Government.

Hallegatte, Stephane. 2014. *Natural Disasters and Climate Change: An Economic Perspective*. Berlin: Springer International Publishing.

Hashizume, Masahiro, Ashraf M. Dewan, Toshihiko Sunahara, M. Ziaur Rahman, and Taro Yamamoto. 2012. Hydroclimatological variability and dengue transmission in Dhaka, Bangladesh: a time-series study. *BMC Infectious Diseases*. 12: p. 98.

He, Zhiguo, Chang-Tai Hsieh, and Zheng (Michael) Song. 2020. COVID-19 Thematic Report No.1: Preliminary Estimates of Economic Effect of Lockdown in China. *COVID-19 Thematic Report No. 1*. Chinese University of Hong Kong – Tsinghua University Joint Research Center for Chinese Economy.

Hyland, Marie and Jason Russ. 2019. Water as Destiny—The Long-term Impacts of Drought in Sub-Saharan Africa. *World Development*. 115 (C): pp. 30–45.

International Monetary Fund. 2021. *World Economic Outlook Update, January 2021*. Washington, DC.

Kahn, Matthew E. 2005. The Death Toll from Natural Disasters: The Role of Income, Geography, and Institutions. *Review of Economics and Statistics*. 87 (2): pp. 271–284.

Karim, Azreen and Ilan Noy. 2016. Poverty and Natural Disasters— A Qualitative Survey of the Empirical Literature. *Singapore Economic Review*. 61 (1): 1640001.

Kocornik-Mina, Adriana, Thomas K. J. McDermott, Guy Michaels, and Ferdinand Rauch. 2020. Flooded Cities. *American Economic Journal: Applied Economics*. 12 (2): pp. 35–66.

Lloyd-Jones, Tony. 2006. *Mind the Gap! Post-Disaster Reconstruction and the Transition from Humanitarian Relief*. London: Royal Institute of Chartered Surveyors.

Lu, Xianfu. 2019. Building Resilient Infrastructure for the Future: Background Paper for the G20 Climate Sustainability Working Group. *ADB Sustainable Development Working Paper Series* No. 61. Manila: Asian Development Bank (July).

Mechler, Reinhard and Stefan Hochrainer-Stigler. 2019. Generating Multiple Resilience Dividends from Managing Unnatural Disasters in Asia: Opportunities for Measurement and Policy. *ADB Economics Working Paper Series* No. 601. Manila: ADB (December).

Mehta, Anouj and Naeeda Crishna Morgado. 2020. Build green to help fend off the next pandemic. *Asian Development Blog*. 6 May.

Miguel, Edward and Gerard Roland. 2011. The Long-Run Impact of Bombing Vietnam. *Journal of Development Economics*. 96 (1): pp. 1–15.

Nakata, Hiroyuki, Yasuyuki Sawada, and Naoki Wakamori. 2020. Robustness of Production Networks Against Economic Disasters: Thailand Case. In Anbumozhi, Venkatachalam, Fukunari Kimura, and Shandremugan Thangavelu (eds). *Supply Chain Resilience*. Singapore: Springer.

Organisation for Economic Co-operation and Development. Query Wizard for International Development Statistics. https://stats.oecd.org/qwids/ (accessed 28 September 2020).

OurWorldInData.org.

Park, Albert and Sangui Wang. 2017. Benefitting from Disaster? Public and Private Responses to the Wenchuan Earthquake. *World Development*. 94 (C): pp. 38–50.

Park, Cyn-Young and Ancilla Marie Inocencio. 2020. COVID-19, Technology, and Polarizing Jobs. *ADB Brief* No. 147. Manila: Asian Development Bank.

Park, Cyn-Young and Kwanho Shin. 2020. The Impact of Nonperforming Loans on Cross-Border Bank Lending: Implications for Emerging Market Economies. *ADB Brief* No. 136. Manila: ADB.

Patankar, Archana. 2019. Impacts of Natural Disasters on Households and Small Businesses in India. *ADB Economics Working Paper Series* No. 603. Manila: ADB (December).

Roser, Max, Hannah Ritchie, Esteban Ortiz-Ospina, and Joe Hasell. 2021. Coronavirus Pandemic (COVID-19). Published online at OurWorldInData. org. Retrieved on 18 January from https://ourworldindata.org/coronavirus.

Sawada, Yasuyuki. 2007. The impact of natural and manmade disasters on household welfare. *Agricultural Economics.* 37 (s1): pp. 59–73.

Sawada, Yasuyuki. 2017. Disasters, Household Decisions, and Insurance Mechanisms: A Review of Evidence and a Case Study from a Developing Country in Asia. *Asian Economic Policy Review.* 12 (1): pp. 18–40.

Sawada, Yasuyuki and Yoshito Takasaki. 2017. Natural Disaster, Poverty, and Development: An Introduction. *World Development* 94 (C): pp. 2–15.

Shinozaki, Shigehiro. 2020. The COVID-19 Impact on Micro, Small, and Medium-Sized Enterprises: Evidence from Rapid Surveys in Indonesia, the Lao People's Democratic Republic, the Philippines, and Thailand. In Bambang Susantono, Yasuyuki Sawada, and Cyn-Young Park (eds). *Navigating COVID-19 in Asia and the Pacific.* Manila: ADB.

Strobl, Eric. 2019. The Impact of Typhoons on Economic Activity in the Philippines: Evidence from Nightlight Intensity. *ADB Economics Working Paper Series* No. 589. Manila: ADB (July).

Surminski, Swenja and Thomas Tanner (eds). 2016. *Realising the 'Triple Dividend of Resilience': A New Business Case for Disaster Risk Management.* Berlin: Springer.

Susantono, Bambang. 2020. Pandemic highlights the need to manage Asia's debt problem. *Asian Development Blog.* 31 March.

Susantono, Bambang, Yasuyuki Sawada, and Cyn-Young Park. 2020. Navigating COVID-19 in Asia and the Pacific. Manila: ADB.

Takenaka, Aiko, James Villafuerte, Raymond Gaspar, and Badri Narayanan. 2020. COVID-19 Impact on International Migration, Remittances, and Recipient Households in Developing Asia. *ADB Brief* No. 148. Manila: ADB.

United Nations Office for Disaster Risk Reduction. 2011. *Global Assessment Report on Disaster Risk Reduction 2011: Revealing Risk, Redefining Development.* Oxford, United Kingdom.

United Nations Office for Disaster Risk Reduction. 2017. *Words into Action Guidelines: Build Back Better in Recovery, Rehabilitation and Reconstruction – Consultative Version.* Geneva.

Wong, Grace. 2008. Has SARS infected the property market? Evidence from Hong Kong. *Journal of Urban Economics.* 63 (1): pp. 74–95.

World Bank. 2012. *Thai Flood 2011: Rapid Assessment for Resilient Recovery and Reconstruction Planning.* Bangkok.

World Bank and United Nations. 2010. *Natural Hazards, UnNatural Disasters: The Economics of Effective Prevention.* Washington, DC.

www.ingramcontent.com/pod-product-compliance
Lightning Source LLC
Chambersburg PA
CBHW040143270326
41928CB00023B/3339